CW01370135

How Good Can You Stand It?

Flourishing Mental Health through Understanding The Three Principles

(Formerly, "Falling in Love with Life")

Thomas Kelley

authorHOUSE

AuthorHouse™
1663 Liberty Drive
Bloomington, IN 47403
www.authorhouse.com
Phone: 1 (800) 839-8640

© 2016 Thomas Kelley. All rights reserved.

No part of this book may be reproduced, stored in a retrieval system, or transmitted by any means without the written permission of the author.

Published by AuthorHouse   12/28/2015

ISBN: 978-1-5049-6422-7 (sc)
ISBN: 978-1-5049-6420-3 (hc)
ISBN: 978-1-5049-6421-0 (e)

Library of Congress Control Number: 2015919397

Print information available on the last page.

Any people depicted in stock imagery provided by Thinkstock are models, and such images are being used for illustrative purposes only. Certain stock imagery © Thinkstock.

This book is printed on acid-free paper.

Because of the dynamic nature of the Internet, any web addresses or links contained in this book may have changed since publication and may no longer be valid. The views expressed in this work are solely those of the author and do not necessarily reflect the views of the publisher, and the publisher hereby disclaims any responsibility for them.

Contents

Acknowledgments ix

Foreword xi

Caution! xvii

Chapter 1   Living with the "Mental Flu" and Searching 1

Chapter 2   Our Birthright of Flourishing Mental Health 10

Chapter 3   Grasping Some New Insights 15

Chapter 4   Who You, Me, All of Us "Really Are" 21

Chapter 5   The Three Principles 34

Chapter 6   How Well Do You Know Yourself? 43

Chapter 7   Thought Recognition: Understanding
the Power of Thought 52

Chapter 8   Using the Power of Thought in Your Best Interest 65

Chapter 9   Using the Power of Thought against Yourself 77

Chapter 10 The Truth about Moods 107

Chapter 11 The Truth about Feelings 116

Chapter 12 Deepening Your Understanding 124

Chapter 13 When Everyone Understands! 137

Epilogue: Making a Difference 151

Three Principles Coaching 152

Three Principles Research 152

Three Principles Books and Websites 155

To My Beautiful Angels—Susan
(my "Duck"), Marty, Kathy and Ricky

Acknowledgments

For decades I searched for lasting happiness and well-being. Finally, my search ended. Through understanding *the three principles* that create our psychological lives, I was able to re-kindle and sustain my birthright of *flourishing* mental health! Writing this book was a labor of love. I want to acknowledge some of the wonderful people who coached me along the way.

David Burns, Wayne Dyer, Albert Ellis and Robert Harper whose writings helped me glimpse the connection between thought and psychological experience.

Landmarke Education Corporation, whose courses helped me distinguish living life in the moment from living life in a thought created story.

Mr. Sydney Banks for uncovering the three principles and sharing them with the world!

Rick Suarez, Roger Mills and Darlene Stewart whose groundbreaking book, *Sanity, Insanity, and Common Sense* first exposed me to the new understandings that later became known as the three principles.

Joe Bailey, Dicken Bettinger, Keith Blevens, Sandy Krot, Ami Chen Mills, Clytee Mills, Linda Pettit, William Pettit, Jack Pransky, Carol Ringold, Rita Shuford, Jeff Timm, and Gordan Trockman whose wise words and writings helped me deepen my understanding of the three principles.

Roger Mills for his wise, kind, patient, invaluable coaching and generous introduction to this book.

Judy Sedgeman, George Pransky and Jack Pransky for their unrelenting commitment to the integrity of the three principles and their generous support and guidance.

My colleagues—Dan Kennedy, Dennis Grifka, Terry Myers, Lewis Smith, Al Yezbick, Steven Stack, Randy McClure, Michael Govan, Lydia Bolen, Cathy Tomilenko and Eric Lambert for their insightful suggestions and enthusiastic support.

My dear friends—Dan, Shirley, Jan, Wally, Dennis, Rena, Manolo, Ingrid, Vito, Roseanna, Terry, Donna, Doug, Judy, Lew, Karen, Butch, Mike and Faith for putting up with my "ego" and loving me anyway.

The thousands of clients and students with whom I have shared the three principles and who helped me deepen my understanding.

My beautiful angels—Susan (my "Duck"), Marty, Kathy and Ricky. Thank-you for your unconditional love, kindness and support. I love you!

Foreword

I want to express my gratitude for Tom Kelley's efforts in writing this book. Although Tom is a tenured professor at Wayne State University and a licensed psychologist, he has never rested on his laurels. He has stayed open and respectful of new ideas. He has not acted as though his accomplishments in the field of psychology privileged him to feel satisfied or to assume he had all the answers. In 1989, he was exposed to the outcomes of several pilot programs conducted in collaboration with residents of inner city communities in Miami. In these communities, the Three Principles intervention had been used as the foundation for resident empowerment and community revitalization efforts. Looking as a researcher at the outcomes of these programs, Tom responded with a refreshing openness and insatiable curiosity. He became committed to understanding why these results were far beyond those achieved from other models of empowerment. He observed leadership, motivation and levels of self-esteem in these communities that he could see would benefit people in all walks of life.

Since then he has studiously applied himself to grasping the impact and potential of these discoveries for the fields of criminal justice and psychology. Although a respected academic and oft published author of professional journal articles, Tom was not satisfied with just an intellectual understanding of new ideas in the field. He sincerely wanted these discoveries to benefit himself, in terms of his own growth and happiness. He realized very deeply the truth of the admonition, "physician heal thyself," recognizing that he could not help others find deeper levels of mental health unless he himself could see substantive changes in this direction *in his own* psychological functioning. He had the humility and dedication to his field to become a serious student of the Three Principles. Over the last several years, while he studiously applied himself to grasping these principles, I have come to admire his willingness to question his thinking at every juncture, and to look, from a deeper vantage point, at things that he felt had previously helped him in life.

His journey is documented in this book. In addition to the case studies used to demonstrate the kinds of changes that result from the logic and power of this approach, Tom was willing to share his own examples. His stories of this own life experiences illustrate how these findings about the nature of our moment to moment mental processes can help us all find deeper levels of happiness, and can allow anyone to achieve a wiser, more understanding perspective on life. His willingness to utilize these insights in his life has allowed him to write a self-help book that can assist the reader find what Tom has found for himself.

The Case of Change and Human Nature

The findings reported in this text provide fascinating clues to less personal, broader facts about human nature and change. They offer a more generic understanding of how we all "tick" psychologically. Recognizing these common denominators as factual, as applying across cultures and personality types or life styles, automatically triggers a process of personal evolution and change. This process is one that moves us continually toward increased well-being and mature healthy thinking. The discovery of these truths has had the benefit of making the personal growth process more genuine, while less personal, far easier and more invigorating. Applying these principles in our personal lives becomes a delightful journey of discovery, one much different than "working on" ourselves. The tone of delight and enthusiasm of this book reflects Tom's excitement of making this discovery, a realization that has now motivated thousands of professionals and researchers to explore and understand these findings more fully.

The True Catalyst for Change

Historically, the early focus in psychology was on identifying pathology and on analyzing past traumas. As a consequence, the field of psychology placed more importance on our negative thinking and emotions, on catharsis, on "dealing with" our problems and hang-ups. The discoveries leading to the new Three Principles understanding have shown us just the opposite. The real power for change lies in the direction of deeper, more natural, more forgiving, more gratifying, more compassionate and loving feelings. These qualities of feelings emerge first for ourselves and then toward others as we recognize that we are all in the same boat. These higher quality, deeper feelings; feelings that stem of our "free flowing," wiser mode of thought, are actually the real catalysts for change. This book points the reader toward both a recognition and unleashing of these qualities of feelings and perceptions.

One of the truths recognized by Tom, reported here in an extremely helpful way, stemmed from his earlier participation in various self-help and personal growth movements. He realized that well-meaning people had, inadvertently, been looking in a misleading direction to accomplish stress reduction or to create positive change. The focus on people's personal thoughts, emotions and past experiences obscured deeper truths and principles of human nature and human functioning. As Tom points out very clearly in this book, to recognize and benefit from these deeper truths, we must first move away from too much of a focus on our personal thoughts and emotions. Putting these emotions and thoughts in a broader perspective allows change to occur without having to work through all of our past, without having to constantly confront or manipulate our thinking or our current difficulties. We can go directly into a healthier mode of thought that bypasses the qualities of thought and affect that got us in trouble in the first place.

The Gift of Thought

As human beings, we were granted the ability to breathe. We have a physical immune system. We have the ability to digest food for energy and other natural health maintenance or health enhancing capacities. We were also given the gift of thought. The explorations leading to the Three Principles understanding convinced us that the gift of thought is the most powerful capacity of any in our repertoire of inborn faculties as human beings. Understanding how to use this gift in the way it was meant to be used is perhaps the most beneficial outcome anyone could realize from this book.

In our work over the last twenty years, these discoveries have been applied across cultures, across diagnoses and across settings with equally positive outcomes. Our appreciation of the ability of individuals in all walks of life to benefit and change from this understanding was strengthened immensely by the extent of growth in clients of clinical, organizational and community based projects conducted over the last thirty years. The majority of people studied in these programs moved from being largely incapacitated, highly dependent clients to becoming healthy, productive citizens. The scope of these results has been amply documented in demonstration programs from Miami, to the South Bronx, in Hawaii and throughout the mid-west, to Oakland, CA and South Central Los Angeles.

The Depth of the Human Potential

This wide variety of applications has shown, in a compelling way, the true depth and promise of the human potential. I am certainly more thrilled and more respectful than ever as the fruits of this understanding multiply, and continue to get stronger after thirty years. I observe the depth of this potential in everyone because I see it unfolding daily in my work. At times, in this book, what Tom is pointing the reader toward seems almost too idealistic, unachievable or unrealistic. I now know with certainty that, at the very least, we all can achieve a relatively stress free, enjoyable, fruitful and richer life that, at the same time, contributes to the well-being of others. This potential and much more, exists as a very natural state of mental functioning in all of us. It is always responsive when we realize how to tap into it. Once tapped, it continues to unfold naturally throughout our lives in an almost magical way.

In this book, Tom has presented these ideas and findings in a down to earth manner. His writing style is direct, it is easy to understand, and eminently graspable. As a result, the reader can quickly apprehend the import and usefulness of his ideas. He has been successful at expressing himself in a clear, common sense fashion. This book was not intended as an academic treatise or more theoretical exploration of these Principles. While it possesses some limitations in this respect, it is true to its purpose. Its purpose is to help people have a nicer, more fulfilling life; to better fulfill their potential as loving, wise and stable human beings. It will, I am sure, greatly assist lay readers to find more happiness, vastly reduce stress and live a more rewarding, satisfying and contented life.

Roger C. Mills, Ph.D.

CAUTION!

Please Read before Proceeding

––––––––––––––––––––––––

Please read this book at your own risk! The *three principles* described herein—when deeply understood—may be hazardous or even fatal to your "ego." If you choose to proceed and grasp these principles at a deep level, you may realize and sustain so much happiness and well-being that your "ego" may disappear! Your desire to "look good," "to be right" and "to prove your self-worth" may dissolve. There may be a striking reduction in conflict in your relationships. You may put the past back in the past and start living more fully in the present! You may even fall "head over heels" in love with life!

I have no gimmicks—no tricks up my sleeve—no false promises—no empty tunnels—no rugs to pull out from under you. If you are willing to consider what's ahead with a curious mind, you will discover—for yourself—how to realize and sustain your birthright of flourishing mental health! When you grasp the new insights waiting for you on our journey, you will discover— just like I did—**how good you can stand it!**

Chapter 1

Living with the "Mental Flu" and Searching

I used to be "normal." Like most people, I had gotten so used to living with the "mental flu"—I thought it was "normal." For years, I did everything I thought was supposed to bring people lasting happiness and well-being. I had a Ph.D., an attractive condominium, a shiny red convertible, a pretty girlfriend, money in the bank, a professorship at a major research university and a thriving psychotherapy practice. Yet—even with all the "right stuff"—my moments of happiness and well-being were fleeting.

I also had a great self-image. Actually—most of the time—"it" had me. I prided myself on being attractive, intelligent, serious, articulate, ambitious and successful. Most of the people who knew me as my "image" thought I had it made. Those who knew me better, however, could see beneath the facade. They saw what I knew was there, but for the life of me couldn't shake—a lot of anxiety and self-consciousness that followed me around like my own shadow.

I was "gripped" by these uncomfortable feelings much of the time. Often, they were attached to my physical appearance—to how I thought I looked. I was compulsive about my hair being perfect—hated windy days—had favorite "check myself out" mirrors in the places I frequented. I hated this lousy habit but couldn't seem to break it.

I also felt a tremendous need to prove my worth by out-performing my peers. At one point, I had seven different jobs at the same time! I prided myself on this achievement. Nonchalantly, I would boast to my friends about balancing these jobs and thought they were pretty impressed. Years later, I asked some of them what they really thought. The typical response, "We thought you were a little crazy." They were right!

During those crazy days, I woke up most mornings with butterflies in my stomach, a lump in my throat and a nervous cough that would come and go. At social events, I would compare my accomplishments to those of my peers and gauge my place in the pecking order. If I ranked myself below number one, I felt anxious and depressed and started thinking up new goals to conquer.

In my relationships, I couldn't make a commitment. I always found a fatal flaw—some terminal imperfection—in every woman I dated. At first, I would try to fix her. When one flaw got fixed I would find another and try to fix it. Eventually, my partner would get fed up and "dump me!" Then, I would be "crushed" and try desperately to get her back. When it was clear that a relationship was over, I would be depressed for months.

By the time I was thirty-two, I had been divorced twice and decided to try some therapy. My therapist was a brilliant man trained in the Neo-Freudian perspective. I usually felt anxious in his reception room, waiting for him to open the door from the hallway to his office. Eventually, his head would appear around the side of the door nodding at me with a faint smile—it was my turn!

Dr. Cowan was formal and serious. He rarely shared anything personal except on one occasion when he exclaimed proudly, "I've been doing psychotherapy for over ten years and the average burnout time for most therapists is five years!" Yet, he often looked tired and occasionally became so drowsy he had to fight to keep his eyes open.

During our sessions we focused on my past—my childhood—my family dynamics. We analyzed my insecure feelings, dreams, divorces and compulsive habits. We did this weekly for about eighteen months. Our sessions were intense and I typically felt anxious while we talked. I guess I was afraid that some awful part of me that I'd never seen before was going sneak out and scare the "bejesus" out of me! When our sessions ended I felt many different ways—confused, sad, relieved—sometimes inspired.

I felt somewhat better after completing therapy—a little less compulsive and perfectionistic—a bit more self-confident. Yet, I had no idea what happened that made this difference. I had little insight into why my mental health went up a notch or two and how to maintain it. More importantly, I still wasn't where I wanted to be. I still didn't have the understandings necessary to experience happiness and well-being as a way of life.

During therapy, I started reading self-help books. Most were grounded in the cognitive-behavioral perspective which challenged the commonly held notion that people's feelings and perceptions are caused by their circumstances, situations and how other people treat them. Instead, this model proposed that people's feelings and perceptions are caused by their beliefs about the events, circumstances and people in their lives.

For me, there was something liberating in this new perspective. I spent considerable time—as these books directed—uncovering, challenging and refuting my irrational beliefs. I worked diligently at thinking more rationally and began using this approach with my psychotherapy clients.

This new understanding made a difference for me—my mental health shot up several notches. Yet, something was still missing. When I was in an unpleasant mood, for example, I found it difficult to try to think more rationally. During my down times, I didn't feel much like challenging my irrational beliefs. While the thought reconditioning tools of cognitive psychology helped me cope better with insecure moods and painful feelings, I still wasn't spending much time feeling content, peaceful and fulfilled. Some important understandings were still missing.

The following summer I was searching in the self-help section of another bookstore. I finally purchased a paperback about a controversial group training that was popular at the time. While reading this book I had a new insight. I realized that I had spent much of my life being "an impostor." I realized that I had made up a story about myself and my life that I thought was "the truth." It dawned on me that I had lived much of my life as if I was a character in a make believe story that I had concocted in my own mind!

Anxious to deepen this new insight, I enrolled in the next available training. Back then, these trainings were held in hotel ballrooms. I can't remember the name of the hotel, but I'll never forget what happened the night before the first training day. Shortly after checking in, three large cold sores erupted on my lower lip!

You can imagine how this went over for someone who thought that his appearance had to be flawless. The very next morning I would be sitting in a brightly lit hotel ballroom with around two hundred strangers—WITH THREE HUGE COLD SORES! After a mild panic attack, I rushed to a nearby drugstore and bought the strongest cold sore medication I could find. Back in my room, I basted those critters most of the night. The medicine didn't faze them!

The next morning I devised a way to camouflage all three cold sores with a sheer, skin-colored Band-Aid. Fortunately, even I had enough sense to realize that the Band-Aid was more conspicuous than the blisters. Finally, I self-consciously dragged myself into the training room—nonchalantly covered my mouth with my hands as much as possible—avoided eye contact with the other trainees. Hey, I did the best I could! Anyway, as the training proceeded, I pretty much forgot about the cold sores and started feeling "normal" again.

Our trainer was extremely confrontational. He berated us—lectured incessantly—put us through several closed-eyed processes—had intense interactions with participants who were brave enough to raise their hand. Some of his techniques were pretty strange. For example, we had to imagine rappelling down the inside of a giant strawberry! Initially, many trainees were frightened, confused, bored—even outraged!

By the end of the training, however, some amazing transformations seemed to occur. Many trainees appeared to experience marked improvement in their mental health. Several participants seemed to make more progress in just the two weekends than most of my "successful" psychotherapy clients after months, even years of therapy!

Several trainees contacted their parents, siblings, children—even ex-spouses—told them how much they loved them—apologized for past hurts, betrayals and abuses. Others appeared to let go of debilitating grudges they had kept alive for five, ten, twenty—even thirty years or more! Several others reported changes of heart about their marriages and declared unwavering commitments to improving them.

In just two weekends, many participants appeared to put the past back in the past and resolve long-held complaints, problems, issues, grudges and resentments. I called my mother and sister after the training and told them how much I loved and appreciated them with more intimacy than I had ever before mustered.

The rapid and dramatic shifts in mental health that seemed to occur for me and many other trainees led me to question many of my core beliefs about how people work psychologically and how they change. Yet, I had no idea how this training worked. For the life of me I couldn't figure out the source of the striking bursts of mental health that I and many other trainees seemed to experience.

Following this training, I participated in several seminars available to graduates. While I seemed to get value from these classes, a confusing thing began to happen. I found myself drifting back into my old self-defeating, perfectionistic habits and anxious feelings. Not as intense as before perhaps, but still annoying and perplexing. I figured that I had lost something that I had initially gained from the training. By participating in additional seminars, I hoped to find "it" again. Occasionally, the original feelings of well-being and vitality would return—but they would soon fade away. To my dismay, something was still missing. I still didn't have the realizations necessary to sustain happiness and well-being as a way of life!

My Missing Breakthrough

The following spring—guess where I was? That's right—in the book section at a discount drugstore looking for another self-help book to read on a trip to Florida. I saw a title that intrigued me—*Sanity, Insanity, and Common Sense.* This book offered a new explanation of people's psychological lives. It was my first exposure to a new understanding that today is commonly known as *the three principles.* I'm not sure why, but I realized then that the insights available to people via understanding the three principles represented a paradigm shift—a true breakthrough for the field of psychology!

The three principles explained every state of mind I had ever experienced. They made sense of every emotion I'd ever felt. They clarified why at times I was stuck in anger and resentment and how, at other times, I felt compassion, respect and love for just about everything.

These three principles accounted for the times I became defensive, irrational and emotionally unstable as well as my more hopeful, inspired and creative moments. They made sense of my every behavior, from the most foolish and self-destructive to the wisest and most responsive. The most complex human problems and conditions appeared to be explained by the three principles! More importantly, this understanding helped me "see" that everyone has all the mental health they need already inside of them!

I began teaching the three principles to my therapy clients. The clients who grasped these principles at a deep level moved from merely coping with life to living with more ease, contentment and exhilaration. They experienced genuine self-esteem, wisdom and common sense. They saw wise—often creative—solutions to their own problems.

The three principles became a major focus of my university teaching and research. I soon noticed more interest, enthusiasm and attention from my students. Many of my criminal justice students, for example, gained a new perspective on crime and delinquency. They began to see the innocence in the behavior of juvenile and adult offenders and to take their misguided behavior less personally.

I began writing research articles applying the logic of the three principles to at-risk youth, delinquency, criminality, trauma, domestic violence and child abuse and neglect. My hope and vision for reducing these and other social problems skyrocketed!

Through understanding the three principles, I finally grasped the missing pieces of the puzzle of realizing and sustaining flourishing mental health! I finally understood how we all work psychologically. I realized how I innocently drifted away from my flourishing mental health birthright and became "normal"—another human being living with the "mental flu" and searching. The three principles pointed me toward these new insights in a gentle, compassionate way. No confrontation, no gimmicks, no New Age malarkey, no struggle, no tools, no techniques, no willpower—no cold sores!

Through understanding the three principles at a deep level, I realized that everyone can realize and sustain flourishing mental health as a lifestyle. The new insights I gained via understanding these principles allowed me to "think like a kid" again and spend more time experiencing the joy, exhilaration and spontaneity that I typically experienced as a young child. Why am I so sure? Well for one thing, I haven't taken a self-improvement course or visited the self-help section of a bookstore *to get better* since!

Chapter 2

Our Birthright of Flourishing Mental Health

Let me be straight with you right from the start. What's in store for you here is not another gimmick, short term fix or empty promise. I know that many of you have read other self-help books. Heaven knows I have—mountains of them! I used to be a self-help book junkie. I learned scores of tools and techniques that helped me cope with the "mental flu." No matter how many books I read, however, some key pieces of the puzzle of realizing and sustaining flourishing mental health were not to be found!

This book is about those missing pieces. Once I discovered them, everything fell into place—I finally realized how we all work psychologically. More importantly, I realized how to tap in to and sustain the flourishing mental health that's alive and well within all of us. These realizations transformed my life. At last I can say without flinching, "I'm a happy man!" Finally, I can declare with a straight face, "I'm in love with life!"

That's why I waited until now to write this book. I've starting writing a self-help book on several occasions. I could never finish one, however, because I knew deep in my soul that I wasn't that happy. How could I coach other people about happiness if I wasn't truly happy? I couldn't do it!

Now, things are different. Now there are times when I'm bursting at the seams with so much exhilaration, wonder, love and gratitude—I can hardly stand it! Now I can honestly declare that I know what's possible for all of us in the arena of flourishing mental health. More importantly, I finally realize the source of flourishing mental health and how to sustain it.

I have no gimmicks—no tricks up my sleeve—no false promises—no empty tunnels—no rugs to pull out from under you. If you are willing to consider what's ahead with a curious mind, you will discover—for yourself—how to realize and sustain your birthright of flourishing mental health! When you grasp the new insights waiting for you on our journey, you will discover—just like I did—*how good you can stand it!*

The Innocent Failure of Psychology

Psychology has produced scores of theories and thousands of studies in its attempt to better understand how we all work psychologically and improve our mental health. Why then, with all of psychology's theories and studies, has there not been a significant improvement in our mental health? If psychology was on the right track, shouldn't our mental health today be better than ever?

On average, people today are physically healthier and live longer. Yet, it's hard to make the case that people's mental health today is better than ever. Take stress, for example. Experts estimate the annual economic cost of stress at over 500 billion dollars! Add to that our skyrocketing rates of divorce, crime, delinquency, bullying, family violence, drug abuse, teen pregnancy, suicide, school drop-out, psychosomatic illness, racism, sexism, work place violence, job dissatisfaction, alcoholism, sexual dysfunction, anxiety, and depression and on and on. Phew! I don't mean to bring you down, but the evidence seems clear that the mental health of most people today is far from optimal.

Even our mental health professionals suffer from high stress levels. Research specific to mental health providers finds that between 21 and 67 percent experience high levels of "burn-out." Dr. Joe Bailey, a three principles psychologist, reports that the typical substance abuse counselor lasts about 2.3 years in each job and "burns out" within five years. When Joe asks them why they quit they typically respond, "The job was just too stressful—I had to get out or crack up!"

What's going on here? What's wrong with this picture? It appears that all of psychology's theories and studies have failed to lead us to improved mental health. Corey Keyes, a major contributor to "positive psychology," concludes that less than one in five people experience optimal or "flourishing" mental health! While around 50% of adults have moderate mental health, Keyes emphasizes that "flourishing people" function markedly better than all others:

> "…flourishing—reported …the healthiest psychosocial functioning (i.e., low helplessness, clear goals in life, high resilience, and high intimacy), the lowest risk of cardiovascular disease, the lowest number of chronic physical diseases, the fewest health limitations of activities of daily living, and lower health care utilization. However, the prevalence of flourishing is barely 20% of the adult population…If

> 'almost there' is good enough, the current approach… is succeeding, because approximately one half of the adult population is moderately mentally healthy. However, because genuine mental health should be the goal, the current approach to national mental health is a failure, because only 17% of adults are completely mentally healthy."

Why are so few people "flourishing?" I don't think that psychology intended this to happen. It appears to me that psychology has done the best it can considering that it hasn't realized the principles that explain how we all work psychologically. How can psychology help us realize and sustain flourishing mental health if it doesn't understand the principles that explain our psychological lives? If you don't understand how something works—how can you get it to work in an optimal way?

If most mental health experts don't understand the principles that explain our psychological lives, then most of us are in for a bumpy journey through life. When people don't understanding how their psychological lives are created, they spend big chunks of time lost in a maze of confusing, misguided ideas about who they are—how they work—where flourishing mental health comes from. They innocently look for happiness and well-being in the wrong places—places that psychology tells them are "related" to happiness—but that innocently point them in the wrong direction. Absent a deep understanding of the principles that explain our psychological lives, psychology is innocently preventing us from realizing and sustaining our flourishing mental health birthright!

The Principles Have Been Uncovered!

Now here's some great news! The principles necessary to unleash a mental health breakthrough are here. Three principles that explain how we all work psychologically have been uncovered. These principles explain why people get upset—why some people are frightened by things that don't frighten others—why negative past events plague many people in the present—why it's hard for some people to tolerate change—why people react differently to the same event—why life seems horribly painful sometimes and absolutely wonderful at other times—why happiness seems to occur at random for many of us—why seemingly "sane" people can suddenly "snap"—why some people get over things quickly while others seem to stay stuck in stress and discontent forever!

The three principles explain every state of mind—every feeling—every perception—that people experience. They make sense of people's every behavior from the wisest to the most foolish. These three simple—yet profound—principles provide the answers to mankind's deepest questions about the mysteries of life. **How good can you stand it?**

Chapter 3

Grasping Some New Insights

The key to realizing and sustaining flourishing mental health is grasping some new insights through understanding the three principles. Realizing and sustaining flourishing mental health doesn't take effort or willpower. It doesn't require adversity, struggle or pain. You don't have to experience negativity, frightening feelings or bad memories to unleash it. You don't have to meditate—recondition your thinking—practice positive affirmations—get in touch with your "inner child"—wade through your past. Forget about confronting or forgiving someone who abused you. You don't have to join a support group. You don't have to build up your ego or self-image. You don't have to scream—beat up on some pillows—have a catharsis! All you have to do to realize and sustain flourishing mental health is grasp some new insights via understanding the three principles.

Imagine that you have taken the same route to work for ten years and think that it's the very best way. What if I showed you another way that was faster, safer—even more scenic! Would it take a lot of effort or struggle for you to switch to the new way? Would you stick with your old route just to "be right" or to avoid looking foolish for taking the old way for so long? Probably not! If you saw—for yourself—that the new way was truly faster, safer and more scenic—you would likely start using it immediately. While you might feel a little sheepish for not seeing the new way sooner, this feeling would quickly pass and you would be "happy as a clam" with the better way!

Imagine that our journey through life is like driving a car down the road. What if we all were taught to steer our "life vehicles" using the rear view mirror instead of the steering wheel! How would this "steering misunderstanding" impact our ability to successfully navigate life? We would think that we were steering in the right direction and then—we would crash! Every now and then—when life's road happened to match our steering—we would reach our desired destination. More often than not, however, after steering very carefully—the rug would be pulled out from under us. We would seldom end up in places that we envisioned!

Imagine what might happen after years of steering through life in this misguided way? We might start driving very slowly to lengthen the time between collisions. We might ask someone else to drive for us so we could blame them for crashing. We might decide that crashing is good and strengthens our character. We might join a self-help support group for "dysfunctional steerers." We might stop driving altogether, park somewhere and settle for cleaning and waxing our vehicles. We might create an imaginary road in our mind that turns in perfect harmony with our steering. We might just "floor it" and take our chances!

Through the new insights waiting for you on our journey, you will discover a faster, safer, more scenic route to lasting happiness and well-being. More importantly, you will realize how to put your hands on the steering wheel of your psychological life. Imagine what your life would be like if you could clearly see the road to flourishing mental health and had the steering realizations necessary to get there. Well—buckle up—that's exactly where we're headed!

The Nature of New Insights

Let's get moving toward some new insights. I suggest we start with some ways to maximize your chances of grasping a new insight—so if one flutters by it will land on you. First, you are less likely to grasp a new insight if you compare, analyze, judge or evaluate the new ideas that I'm going to share with you. A new insight is less likely to settle in your lap if you deliberately sift these new ideas through what you already know about psychology, happiness, well-being or anything else. So here's my request. Please put on the back burner all the knowledge that you have accumulated so far. If what you already know had led you to lasting happiness and well-being—you probably wouldn't be reading this!

Another fact about insights is that it's virtually impossible to *try* to have one. Insights happen on their own schedule—spontaneously—"out of the blue." When a new insight is good and ready, it shows up—"Aha!" Being willing to have a new insight is helpful. Relaxing your mind—not trying to have one—is more helpful. Why? Because when your mind is "busy" processing or analyzing—the path of a new insight gets blocked. A new insight is more likely to land on your shoulder when your mind is quiet—your heart is light—you have a nice, easy feeling.

Insights are permanent—once you grasp one you can never lose it. During an unpleasant mood it may seem to fade a bit. However, as soon as your mind quiets down your new perspective will re-surface as clear as ever. Once you have a new insight, it's impossible to see life the same way you saw it before.

Here's an example of a new insight that most of us experienced as a young children—riding a two-wheel bicycle for the first time. Riding a "two-wheeler" requires a new insight regarding "balance." Before attempting to ride, we could have gone to the library and studied "balance" for months. Unfortunately, accumulating all the knowledge in the world about balance wouldn't have helped much. In fact, trying to remember what we learned about balance would have made a new "balancing insight" less likely. Balance is an experience that we just had to "experience!"

For me it went something like this. I grabbed the handlebars and pushed my bike forward to gain some momentum. Then, I put my foot on a pedal and threw my other leg over the seat toward the other pedal. Then, the front wheel started wobbling uncontrollably—I tumbled to the ground—skinning both knees and an elbow. I was persistent, however, and repeated this maneuver over and over again until finally—I experienced "BALANCE!" Wow—I was riding! MOM—DAD—LOOK—I'M RIDING! Instantly, I saw a slew of new possibilities unleashed by this new insight—freedom, independence, new places to go, new people to meet, time saved and on and on! Of course, my new "balance insight" was permanent. If I didn't ride again for years, I could find a bike and go. I might be a bit rusty at first—but in no time my transformed relationship with balance would be as good as new.

Listening for New Insights

The best way to maximize your chances of grasping a new insight is to sharpen up your listening. If you are willing to troll through the sea of insights using "powerful listening" as your bait, your chances of hauling in a nice big insight will skyrocket!

First, it's very helpful to listen with humility. This means listening from "outside the box" of what you already know. Some call it "listening for not knowing." This means not trying to fit what's coming into the "stuff" you already know. Why? Because by "listening for not knowing" you free up your inner wisdom to listen for you. By listening intuitively—rather than analytically—you are more likely to hear a new insight. So, be "tortoise mind"—not "hare brain!" Replace analysis with reflection. Check your "ego" at the door and listen with the humility and curiosity of a young child. Allow the new ideas that we will visit to marinate in your inner wisdom.

A Peaceful Journey

Now that you understand the nature of insights and the best way to listen for one, let me assure you that our journey will be peaceful and serene. I know that some of you—like me—have looked for happiness via counseling or psychotherapy. Unfortunately, many psychotherapists believe that people have to get worse before they can get better—have to re-live painful past events—dredge up awful memories of early traumas—no pain-no gain!

Trust me—you don't have to go through negativity to get healthy. Imagine having a migraine headache, going to the doctor and the doctor tells you that to cure your headache he has to give you a little stomach flu! You would high tail it out his door—licitly split!

There is, however, one slightly uncomfortable feeling that would be helpful to experience—feeling foolish! It would be helpful for you to feel foolish every now and then on our journey. Why? Because when you grasp a new insight you will realize that some of your old perspectives were pretty silly. When people realized that the world was round, it soon occurred to them that worrying about falling off the edge was pretty silly. On our journey, however, feeling foolish is good thing—it means that you are catching on—grasping new insights—seeing life in fresh, new ways. So relax—lighten up—listen "for not knowing"—feel foolish as often as possible! **How good can you stand it?**

Chapter 4

Who You, Me, All of Us "Really Are"

I used to be "a searcher." From the semester I took my first psychology class I began trying to "find myself"—to discover "who I really was." I became a regular at the self-help shelves at several local bookstores. I bought loads of self-improvement CD's—listened to countless motivational speakers, spiritual gurus and radio talk shrinks—attended scads of self-improvement courses, seminars and workshops—completed scores of psychotherapy sessions. I was on what seemed like a never-ending expedition to find my "true self" and hopefully more happiness.

Helping people discover "who they really are" is a billion dollar industry. Bookstores, libraries and the internet are loaded with self-help books, classes, CD's, blogs and videos designed to help people "find themselves." Scores of support groups purport to help people unravel their past so they can "get in touch with themselves" and overcome all kinds of bad habits and addictions.

How often have you or someone you know lamented, "I don't know who I am anymore." Most people move in and out of a firm sense of personal identity. One day they think they know who they are—the next day they are not so sure. Some days people feel "in touch with themselves"—other days they feel like impostors.

The first thing that's essential to clear up on our journey is the truth about who you—me—all of us really are. Why? Because when people aren't clear about who they really are, they waste a lot of time feeling out of sync with life as it comes at them point blank in each moment. Like a piano out of tune or a movie out of focus, people's experience of life is fuzzy and discordant to the degree they are confused about and trying to figure out who they really are.

Unfortunately, most people believe a lot of "malarkey" about who they are. Most people believe that their identity is tied to a slew of external factors and circumstances. For example, many people believe that they are "their achievements." When these people achieve at a certain level they feel secure and worthwhile. When they fail to achieve at a particular level, however, they lose their bearings—start doubting themselves—even have a full-blown identity crisis!

Many people think that they are "their feelings." Some people— quick to anger—think that they are volatile—hot-tempered— aggressive people. Other people who feel little empathy or compassion view themselves as cold, uncaring people. Others who feel anxious in social situations think they are insecure—even damaged—people.

Many people believe they are their thoughts, opinions, beliefs and points of view. These individuals think that their worth depends on "being right." When their opinions and viewpoints are challenged— they feel challenged—as if their beliefs and points of view are who they are.

Many people believe that their "traits" define them. Some people become paralyzed if life calls for a trait they don't think they are. Imagine a situation where a bold or assertive response makes perfect sense. However, if the person sees only "shy" on his or her "trait menu," then only a shy or passive response is likely. Ask this person why and you will hear, "That's just me—I'm really shy."

Who you are "Really Not"

In a few moments, I'm going to propose who I "know" you—me—all of us "really are!" What I'm going to assert may startle some of you. I hope, however, that what I posit will convince you—once and for all—to stop your futile search to discover who you really are. You won't have to read anymore self-help books—listen to anymore CDs—take anymore self-improvement classes—attend anymore motivational sessions—at least not to discover who you really are.

Let's begin by exposing some "artificial identities" that I know you are "really not." You may think that you are one or more of these false identities. Your parents, teachers, friends—even a therapist—may have convinced you that you are one or more of these "false selves." Trust me—you really are none of them!

Here goes. You are not your thoughts. You—me—all of us—live in a sea of thought. Your thoughts, however, are not who you are. You are not your feelings. You likely experience a wide range of feelings. Your feelings, however, are not who you are. You are not your beliefs, opinions and points of view—these are merely habits of thinking that you picked up along the way—they are not who you are. You are not your accomplishments. Your achievements are things you have done in life—good for you! However, your accomplishments are not who you are. You are not your traits. You learned each of them with some help from your genes—may have mistaken them for you. I assure you—you are not a bunch of traits! You are not the roles you play in life such as mother, husband, teacher, doctor or boss. When you "came down the chute," these roles were already here—pieces on the game board of life. Some picked you—you picked some others—began playing in the game. However, these roles are not who you are. Last, but not least, you are not a "self-image" or an "ego." These "identity illusions" may be "who you think you are," but they are not really you. In a nutshell—*anything that you think you are—you are not!*

It might be helpful to take a deep breath—relax—let your mind clear. In a few moments I'm going to ask you to try on a new understanding regarding who you—me—all of us—really are. Now that you have considered several "artificial identities" that I am certain you are "really not"—I'm going to ask you to consider who I assert that you—me—all of us "really are."

To make this new understanding easier to for you to grasp, please recall your childhood. Remember when your parents told you about Santa Claus, the Tooth Fairy, the Easter Bunny or some other imaginary characters? Remember when they told you about the eight reindeer flying Santa around on Christmas Eve—Rudolph with his bright red nose leading the pack—the big bunny rabbit hiding colored eggs on Easter morning—the Tooth Fairy waiting to collect your bicuspid and leave some money under your pillow?

As a child, it's likely you thought that some of these mythical figures were real. It's likely that you, like me, "bought into" some of these wonderful fantasies. You thought that some of these imaginary characters actually existed. You might have cared deeply for some of them. Perhaps you left milk and cookies out for Santa on Christmas

Eve—your molar under your pillow for the Tooth Fairy—some carrots for the Easter Bunny and Rudolph.

Now, try to remember how you felt when you realized that these wonderful creatures were "made up!" How did you feel when it finally dawned on you that each one was an illusion, a myth, a fairy tale? How did you feel when you realized that there is no real Santa Claus—no real Easter Bunny—no real Tooth Fairy? How did you feel when you discovered that each one was a joke? Deceived, sad, disappointed—shocked?

Well, please get ready for another reality check. I'll try to make this one as easy for you to handle as possible. I'm sorry to have to tell you this, but somebody has to do it and most of you are old enough to handle the truth. Ready? Here goes. There is no Santa Claus—and you don't have a "true self" out there waiting to be discovered—please stop searching! There is no Tooth Fairy—and you don't have a "real identity" out there waiting to be found—please stop looking! Reindeer can't fly—and you are not a collection of "personality traits"—please stop thinking that you are. There is no Easter Bunny—and you have all the self-esteem, wisdom and well-being you need already inside of you you—please stop working on yourself!

Here's the bottom line. Self, identity, self-image, self-concept, ego, and personality traits are not real things or entities. If we cut you open and looked inside, we would find organs, blood, bones, muscles and tissue—but absolutely none of the above. Why? Because each one is an illusion—make believe—just like Santa and the Easter Bunny. However, like you once did with Rudolph and the Tooth

Fairy, it's likely that you believe that one or more of these "identity illusions" is really you. Well, I'm proposing that none of them is real or true—that you can never find any of them, strengthen any of them or become any of them. I'm absolutely certain that none of them is who you really are!

Each of these "identity illusions" was made up, invented, imagined by some well-intentioned psychologists who were trying their best to understand how people work psychologically. Unfortunately, they were off the mark—didn't realize it at the time—started promoting these "identity myths" innocently believing that they were real or true.

Unfortunately, most people started believing in these "false identities" and guess what—when people believe something—their beliefs look very real to them. When people believe something, they start collecting evidence that appears to support their beliefs. When you believed in Santa Claus and fairies, didn't these mythical characters look absolutely real to you? When people believed that the Earth was flat, it really looked flat to them. No kidding! Well, the same thing has likely occurred for you regarding some of these false identities. They may look real to you—but they are not!

You may have a few questions at this point. You may be wondering, "If I'm not a self, an identity, an ego, a self-concept, my feelings, my thoughts, my beliefs, my accomplishments, my roles, my traits or anything else that I think I am—then who am I? If I don't have a "true self" to discover, an "authentic identity" to find, an ego to prove, a self-image to strengthen, some fixed personality traits to express— then what should I do? If I stop searching for my "true self"—if I quit trying to build up my ego or self-image—if I stop thinking of myself as a fixed personality—then what's left to do?"

These are great questions and the answers will appear to you as we continue our journey toward new insights. When you realize the answers, you will be thrilled with the news that who you really are is none of these "identity illusions."

Who you "Really Are!"

In a moment I'm going to ask you to "try on" who I assert that you—me—all of us—really are. Before I share this new understanding with you, however, please keep listening in the most helpful way. When you first hear what I going to propose, it may sound a little strange. When you first heard that there was no real Santa Claus you may have resisted this news with "all your might." So please remember to listen quietly and avoid judging what I'm about to propose. Keep "listening for not knowing"—let your wisdom decide if what I'm proposing makes sense.

Ready—here goes. **You—me—all of us—are spiritual beings experiencing a human psychological life created "through us" from the "inside-out" via three principles—Universal Mind, Consciousness and Thought.** From the moment we are born until our last breath, our psychological lives—our thoughts, feelings, perceptions, moods—are created "through us" from the "inside-out" by the principles of Universal Mind, Consciousness and Thought. **Mind, Consciousness and Thought are the three principles that all of us "use" to construct and experience our psychological lives.**

None of us is born being a self, an identity, our thoughts, our feelings, our accomplishments, our points of view, our roles, our personality traits, an ego, a self-image—or any other "identity illusion." In the same way that we all "use" the principle of gravity to stay planted firmly on the Earth—we all "use" the principles of Mind, Consciousness and Thought to create and experience our psychological lives! **Who you—me—all of us "really are" is—the three Principles—Mind, Consciousness and Thought—in action!**

Everything is Perfect

Everything in the universe is perfect! Everything that exists and happens in the universe is a perfect expression of *principles— fundamental truths, laws or facts of nature that explain how something works or why something happens.* There are principles that explain tornados, hurricanes and tidal waves. There are principles that account for gravity and electricity. There are principles that explain the operation of every organ and system in the human body. There are principles that account for every human illness and disease. Principles that explain everything in the universe are constantly operating—continually "doing their thing"—whether people realize it or not.

Principles are impersonal. The principles behind tidal waves, for example, don't care if hundreds of people on a beach get swept away. The principle of electricity doesn't care if someone gets shocked or electrocuted. The principle of gravity doesn't care if someone slips off the edge of the Grand Canyon!

Throughout history, the biggest breakthroughs for humankind have occurred when someone uncovers principles. When someone realizes principles—shares his or her realization—the world is eventually transformed! When principles are uncovered and understood, people "see" how certain things really work and are empowered to use these principles in their best interest. When people finally understand principles, there is an explosion—a vertical leap—of positive change in the domain explained by those principles. For example, on average, people live longer today because several principles that explain how the human body works have been uncovered. Today, fewer people are hurt by tornados, hurricanes and tidal waves because scientists better understand the principles that explain these events and can better predict their intensity and trajectory.

The Principles of Psychological Experience

Over a century ago, William James, a principal founder of psychology, predicted that psychology would eventually uncover fundamental principles that explain psychological experience and illuminate a path to improved mental health for everyone. James realized that the principles that explain people's psychological lives have always existed—waiting for someone to uncover them—transform the field of psychology—improve people's mental health! Well—guess what! The principles that explain how we all work psychologically have been uncovered! Not by a psychologist, however. By a common laborer named Sydney Banks! Mental health pioneer, Donald Klein, described Banks's realization:

> "Several years ago, the director of a community mental health center in Oregon…suggested that I

look into the positive effects on people's physical and emotional well-being being achieved by a spiritually enlightened man in British Columbia. A few years before, this man…had suddenly entered into a vastly different level of awareness, a state of understanding and grace, based on no particular religious philosophy or practice, a form of spontaneous spiritual transformation about which William James had written in the early 1900's…his discoveries…were obviously worth exploring from the standpoint of preventive mental health …something very important was taking place…our most basic assumptions about human behavior were being challenged."

Sydney Banks experienced a "spontaneous spiritual transformation" where he ultimately realized that three principles—Universal Mind (or Mind), Consciousness and Thought—account for people's entire psychological experience. Banks "saw" that these three principles are fundamental truths always operating in the psychological realm, much as gravity exists as a principle of the physical world and is always present, whether people know of it or not. Banks asserted that Mind, Consciousness and Thought represent the unifying, undergirding principles for psychology that William James originally envisioned but never realized.

"Using" the Three Principles

You—me—all of us really are, "the three principles in action." You—me—all of us constantly "use" the principles of Mind, Consciousness and Thought to create and experience our psychological lives! I need to be crystal clear regarding what I mean when I say—*we all "use" the three principles.* When I say that we "use" the three principles—*I don't mean that we do anything!* All that's necessary to "use" the three principles is to be "a live human being!" No tools, techniques, beliefs or actions are necessary to "use" the three principles. As soon as we are born (actually from the moment of conception) we start "using" the three principles to create and experience our psychological lives in the same way that we start "using" gravity "to stay put!" As soon as we arrive on Earth, gravity keeps us on firmly planted on the ground with no effort from us and Mind, Consciousness and Thought create our psychological lives— with absolutely no effort on our part! The better we understand the three principles, however, the better we can "use" them to realize and sustain our birthright of flourishing mental health!

Our Flourishing Mental Health Birthright

Virtually all of us are born physically healthy. Physical health is an innate gift—a birthright. Why would it be different regarding mental health? Why wouldn't we also be born with the gift of mental health? What sense would it make for people to be born physically healthy and mentally ill? What an absurd, cruel joke that would be! I don't know about your creator, higher power or intelligence behind life—but mine wouldn't play such a lousy trick on me! The only sensible answer is obvious. *You—me—all of us—are born with all the mental health we need already inside of us!* Even more phenomenal— unlike physical health—mental health is indestructible—nothing can damage it—it is always available to us! When people understand who they really are—the three principles in action—at a deep level—they stop searching and start realizing and sustaining their birthright of flourishing mental health!

Young Children are Great Examples

Young children aren't awake in the middle of the night trying to figure out "who they really are." Young children don't give a hoot about improving a "self-image." They don't spend a lick of time searching for a "true identity." They don't identify with their thoughts, feelings, accomplishments, beliefs or traits. They spend most of their moments being themselves—naturally "using" *the three principles in their best interest*—experiencing flourishing mental health. They wake up most mornings exhilarated and inspired—have boundless energy—absorb knowledge like little sponges—express themselves fully—show love and affection unconditionally—dance and sing spontaneously—rebound from unpleasant moods in no time flat!

How did you typically experience life as a young child? Can you remember any games you created—games that occurred to you from out of the blue? I remember creating a rocket ship under our basement stairs. I draped some blankets over the sides. Some tinker toys became the instrument panel—an old tube-type vacuum cleaner the rocket engine. I was Tom Corbet, space cadet. My friends were my shipmates, Astro and Manning. We explored the galaxies together long before Captain Kirk, Dr. Spock and the rest of the Star Trek crew made the scene. We were totally absorbed in our adventures and enjoyed every moment. We seldom got bored and continued to play until we were struck by a fresh idea. Instantly, a new game got created!

When I was about six, I remember digging a small round hole in the corner of our yard. Then I moved as far away as possible and using a baseball bat as my golf club, hit a softball toward the hole until I rolled it in. I was Arnold Palmer and Jack Nicklaus. I made putts worth thousands of dollars as the crowd roared. I did this for hours on end—enjoyed every whack of the ball—every walk to the hole. I didn't connect my worth to my score. Missing a shot was as fun as making one. I was simply being myself—*the three principles in action*—immersed in flourishing mental health.

Unfortunately, nobody ever told us about the three principles when we were children. So we innocently began drifting away from the rich, clear signal of our flourishing mental health birthright. Wouldn't it be wonderful to get that signal tuned in again as clearly as it was when we were young children? With the new insights waiting for you via understanding yourself—the three principles in action—you will start "thinking like a kid" again and rekindle and sustain your birthright of flourishing mental health. **How good can you stand it?**

Chapter 5

The Three Principles

To help you understand how the three principles create our psychological lives please pretend that you are a movie projector. That's right—to help you grasp how we all "use" the three principles to create and experience our psychological lives—please imagine that you are one of those old fashioned movie projectors—the star of a Disney Studio animated feature.

Take a few moments to get into character. Imagine your main projector parts—your powerful motor—your projection light—your two film reels. Now, find a power outlet and plug yourself in. Okay, flip your switch to the "on" position. Wow! Your projection light is beaming out into space!

Now Mr. or Ms. Movie Projector, please reflect on how you work. If your projection light is working just fine but no film is turning on your reels—what would appear on your screen? That's right—your screen would be empty—no form, no color, no sound. What must be added for your screen to come to life? That's right—some film. With film turning on your reels for your light to project—animate—enliven—your screen will come to life with form, color and sound.

Would it be helpful for you to understand how you and all the other movie projectors work? Well, if your understanding of movie projector functioning is poor, it might appear to you that what shows up on your screen has nothing to do with you. You might think that something or someone "out there" is responsible for what appears on your screen. Also, you might think that everything that appears on your screen is real or true.

On the other hand, if you had read *"How Good Can You Stand It for Movie Projectors"* you would realize that everything that appears on your screen is created "through you" from the "inside-out." You would understand that you are plugged into an energy source that powers your light to enliven your film and make it appear real to you on your screen.

Here are some final questions, Mr. or Ms. "enlightened" movie projector. Is anything that appears on your screen really "real" or "true?" Well, while everything on your screen certainly looks real—the answer is a resounding "NO!" Each frame of film that gets projected simply creates a momentary "illusion." As soon the next frame gets projected, a different illusion—that looks just as real—shows up on your screen.

Would understanding movie projector functioning help you have a more peaceful, satisfying life? I think it would. For one thing, you won't be confused or disturbed when some frightening or depressing film happens to get projected. You will realize that it's "just film"—just some temporary unpleasant illusions. With this understanding, you will be better able to keep your bearings—wait gracefully until these uncomfortable frames pass through.

Also, you will understand why your projector buddies often see things very differently than you see them. You will find this interesting rather than upsetting or frustrating. You won't try to convince them that your projections are right and their projections are wrong. Why? Because you realize that they are illuminating different film that looks just as real to them as your film does to you.

Every now and then, of course, you will be out of focus. I hear that this happens occasionally to even the most enlightened movie projectors. During these times, the quality of your projections will be fuzzy, blurred, drab—even black and white. However, since you understand movie projector functioning at a deep level, you won't be disturbed by these temporary distortions. You won't freeze these painful frames to review and entertain. You won't panic—race to the concession stand—"pig out" on popcorn and gummy bears. No, you will realize that it's merely an unpleasant movie projector mood—just some disheartening film being enlivened by your light. So, you will relax—not take these projections to heart—wait for your built-in refocusing mechanism to kick in and do its job. Soon, your projections will again be crisp and clear!

We Work A Lot Like Movie Projectors!

Believe it or not, we humans work a lot like movie projectors! Like movie projectors—we are plugged into a power source. This "life force" or "life energy" is the first principle—the **principle of Universal Mind** or **Mind**. Mind powers the other two principles—the **principle of Consciousness** and the **principle of Thought.** The principle of Thought refers to our *ability to think*—our ability to create thoughts—mental images—mental pictures in our mind—*our human film.* The principle of Consciousness refers to our capacity to be aware of—to have a sensory experience—of the thoughts that we think—*our human projection light.* Consciousness enlivens our thoughts—projects them onto our psychological screens—makes them appear real to us. You—me—all of us are—the three principles in action!

The Principle of Mind

Mind refers to the purest life force—the source or energy of life itself—the Universal, creative intelligence within and behind life, human beings and the natural world. Mind powers our thinking—our ability to create thoughts, images, pictures, representations of the world in our mind. Mind also powers consciousness—our ability to be aware of—have a sensory experience of the thoughts we think. In sum, Mind mixes thought (our psychological film) with consciousness (our psychological projection light) to create our moment to moment experience (on our psychological screens). Everyone's psychological life is formed in this way— "through them" from the "inside-out." Our psychological lives happen "through us" not "to us." *We can only "know" a psychological life created "through us" from the "inside-out" via Thought plus Consciousness—all powered up by Mind.*

The Principle of Consciousness

Consciousness works much like a movie projector's light beam. Consciousness converts our thoughts into our experience—brings our thoughts to life—makes our thoughts appear real to us. Think about it, when people are unconscious they don't experience their thoughts—a fact much appreciated by me during a recent colonoscopy! Like film running through a movie projector with a burned out projection light, our psychological screens are empty without consciousness to illuminate our thoughts.

Consciousness alone, however, is not enough. Thought has to be mixed with consciousness to create our personal realities. A special effects department can't bring a film to life without a script. Consciousness enlivens our thoughts through our physical senses—sight, sound, touch, smell and taste. To illustrate—please hold old out one hand and imagine I'm handing you a fat, ripe, juicy, yellow lemon. Feel the shape of the plump, juicy lemon—notice its smooth, waxy skin. Bring the lemon up to your nose and savor its lemony scent? Now, please hold out your other hand—I'm handing you a razor sharp kitchen knife. Careful—don't cut yourself! Okay, slice the plump, juicy lemon in half. Look out—some lemon juice just squirted near your eye. Now—quickly—take a big bite of the lemon's glistening, sour pulp. You just experienced the three principles in action. There was no real lemon—just your own "lemony"—or other thoughts—enlivened through your senses via consciousness—all powered up by Mind!

If this example didn't do it for you—imagine some dry chalk screeching on a blackboard. Or try this one—imagine sliding down a long banister that suddenly turns into a razor blade! Sorry—I just want you to realize how your every experience is created "through you" from the "inside-out" via the three principles in action.

People with posttraumatic stress disorder (PTSD)—many war veterans and violent crime victims—occasionally experience flashbacks of a past horrid event. When memories of the event flood their minds, they re-experience the event as if it was happening in the present. Interestingly, most people exposed to the same potential traumatic event—such as those in or near the World Trade Center on 9/11—don't end up with PTSD. This makes perfect sense, however, when one understands that thought plus consciousness—not external events—is the source of people's psychological experience.

People with a "psychosomatic disorder" experience pain or paralysis in a limb or elsewhere for which there is no physical explanation. For these people, their thoughts carry the message of pain to their senses. Most of us have experienced less pain when our thinking gets placed elsewhere. That's how hypnosis works to create a "psychological anesthetic" for surgical procedures and how Lamaze works for natural birthing. When people don't think about pain, consciousness has no painful thoughts to enliven!

The Principle of Thought

Thought refers to our "ability to think"—not "what we think." Thought refers to our ability to create thoughts (psychological film frames) that our consciousness enlivens—brings to life—makes appear real—on our psychological screens. In each moment, our psychological lives—our feelings, our perceptions, our moods—are constructed by the thoughts we think made to look real by our consciousness—all powered up by Mind. Then, *our behavior is perfectly synchronized with our moment-to-moment personal realities being created "through us" from the "inside-out" by our "effortless use" of the three Principles!*

Experiencing an "Outside-In" Life

Occasionally, I ask my university students this question, "Can anyone tell me the source of every one of your feelings, perceptions and moods?" So far, not one student has come up with the correct answer. Their typical responses include present or past circumstances, socialization, temperament, personality traits and heredity.

What's even more concerning, however, is that most mental health professionals can't answer this question with certainty. At last count, there were over four hundred different psychotherapies—each with a different explanation of how people work psychologically—each with a different approach to prevention and treatment. Consider your chances of getting a "sick" car running smoothly again if there were over four hundred different views on how to repair the same engine!

Why is it essential to understand how we all work psychologically? Well, how about this. If you don't understand how something works, then how are you going to use it in your best interest? If you don't understand how something works, then how are you going to fix it if it breaks down? If you don't understand how something works then are you not more likely to misuse it and hurt yourself!

When people don't understand the "inside-out" nature of psychological experience, they tend to live in the illusion that the quality of their lives depends on "stuff out there"—their situations, circumstances and how other people treat them. They tend to believe that their feelings, perceptions and moods are created from the "outside-in." When people don't realize how we all work psychologically, they tend to view external factors as the cause of their psychological lives.

What happens then? Well, when people believe that the quality of their lives depends on "stuff out there," they spend a lot of time "tinkering" with "stuff out there." They get caught up in what I call the "more/better/different" game. Here's how it works. People think that they will be happier when they get *more* "stuff out there" (e.g., money)—get *better* at "stuff out there" (e.g., parenting)—do "stuff out there" in a *different* way (e.g., change jobs).

Unfortunately, the "more/better/different" game can't transport people to sustained mental health. To ego highs and lows—definitely. To identity illusions—certainly. To sustained flourishing mental health—never! Most people don't realize this, however. Why? Because most people don't understand how we all work psychologically and that mental health doesn't come from "stuff out there." So when their first round of "more/better/different" tinkering doesn't result in sustained happiness and well-being—they try again. In the next round, they get more "stuff"—get *better* at "the stuff" they're already doing—do "the stuff" they're doing in a *different* way—and on and on and on and on and on and on!

When people don't understand the "inside-out" nature of people's psychological lives, they innocently look for happiness in empty tunnel after empty tunnel. Why are these tunnels empty? Because it's impossible to sustain happiness and well-being by doing "more/better/different" anything out there. Mental health doesn't come from "stuff out there." Mental health is built into each of us and when people understand the three principles—at a deep level—they realize how to sustain flourishing mental health as a lifestyle.

Unfortunately most people don't have a clue that—in each and every moment—their psychological lives are created "through them" from the "inside-out." Thus, they misguidedly keep searching and searching—playing "more/better/different" over and over—never sustaining the flourishing mental health they crave. Instead, most people spend big chunks of their lives tinkering with the stuff they've collected and stored in their "outside-in" tunnels!

Can you blame people for being seduced by the "more/better/different" game? Of course not! When people don't understand that who they really are is the three principles in action, it appears to them that happiness can be found and maintained by tinkering with "stuff out there." Even when their common sense tries to warn them that they are looking in the wrong direction, most people don't trust their inner wisdom. Most people don't respect their innate wisdom even when it hits them directly "on the noggin." Not trusting their intuition and witnessing countless others hooked on the "more/better/different" game, most people think, "What if my intuition is wrong and my neighbor finds more happiness than me?"

With all due respect—isn't it time to stop tinkering? Unleashing and sustaining flourishing mental health doesn't require effort, struggle or tinkering. You don't have to tinker with anything out there—your job, your spouse, other people, you. You don't have to do "more/better/different" anything out there? All that's necessary is grasping some new insights through understanding who you really are—the three principles in action. When you get to know yourself better—the steering wheel of your psychological life will get planted more firmly in your hands. **How good can you stand it?**

Chapter 6

How Well Do You Know Yourself?

If who you really are is the three principles in action—how well do you know yourself? Are you "using" the principles in your best interest and typically experiencing your birthright of flourishing mental health? Below is a list of "flourishing mental health symptoms." Let's call it—"List A." People with a deep understanding of themselves—the three principles in action—experience these symptoms as a lifestyle. Understanding the three principles at a deep level is all that it takes to reside in "List A." Nothing else is necessary—no tools, no techniques, no beliefs. "List A" represents the psychological community in which you—me—all of us are meant to reside throughout life. Age, gender, ethnicity, religion, occupation, political affiliation, sexual orientation, income and past or present circumstances have absolutely no bearing on whether or not someone resides in "List A." "List A" is an equal opportunity community. However, whether people own there—or merely rent or visit every now and then—depends on how well they know themselves—the three principles in action!

Please take a moment to reflect on the items in "List A." Doing so will help you gauge your understanding of the three principles—help you determine whether you typically "use" the three principles in your best interest—help you realize how well you know yourself—the three principles in action. Please check the column next to each item that best describes how often you experience that item.

"List A"—Symptoms of Flourishing Mental Health

Directions: How often do you experience each of the following?

	Most of the time	Much of the time	Some of the time	Seldom	Hardly ever
1. A clear, peaceful mind					✓
2. Stress-free productivity			✓		
3. Effortless concentration					✓
4. Contentment, well-being					✓
5. Getting over anger easily		✓			
6. Life as an interesting adventure				✓	
7. Well-being during unpleasant moods				✓	
8. Curiosity, inquisitiveness			✓		
9. Being present in the moment			✓		
10. Well-being during difficult circumstances				✓	
11. A sense of humor			✓		
12. Changing your mind easily				✓	
13. Being relaxed, at ease				✓	
14. Insightful, creative				✓	
15. Forgiving yourself and others easily			✓		

		Most of the time	Much of the time	Some of the time	Seldom	Hardly ever
16.	Content with things the way they are				✓	
17.	Wisdom, common sense			✓		
18.	Kindness, generosity		✓			
19.	Not taking unpleasant moods to heart				✓	
20.	Your worth unattached to accomplishments/ possessions	✓				
21.	Joyfulness				✓	
22.	Lightheartedness		✓			
23.	Empathy		✓			
24.	Compassion			✓		
25.	Open-mindedness				✓	
26.	Optimism					
27.	Learning from mistakes and moving on			✓		
28.	Gratefulness		✓	✓		
29.	Love				✓	
30.	**In Love with Life!**					

Let's examine your responses. How often did you check "most of the time" or "much of the time?" If most of your ratings fell in these columns, it would appear that you know yourself pretty darn well—that your understanding of the three principles is pretty deep—that you typically "use" the three principles in your best interest. Congratulations! I request, however, that you stay with us on our journey. Why? Because I'm confident that you can deepen your understanding of the three principles. By continuing to listen "for not knowing," you can realize and sustain greater depths of your flourishing mental health birthright.

On the other hand, if most of your ratings fell in the "some of the time," "seldom," or "hardly ever" categories—you need to get better acquainted with yourself. Your understanding of the three principles has room to grow. Please don't be discouraged—it's not your fault! It's likely that nobody ever told you that who you really is the three principles in action. It's likely that nobody ever pointed you toward the new insights that reveal how to "use" the three principles in your best interest. When people didn't understand the principles of gravity and electricity, many misused them and were innocently hurt. With a few more new insights, you will realize how to allow yourself—the three principles in action—to work in your best interest and move into the community of "List A."

The "Mental Flu"

Did you happen to you notice that several "List A" items reflect the ability to maintain well-being during difficult circumstances and unpleasant states of mind? Flourishing mental health isn't just having positive experiences such as those on "List A." Flourishing mental health also involves recognizing symptoms of the "mental flu" and relating to these symptoms in a way that diffuses their power—hastens their passing—prevents them from becoming "mental pneumonia." This is called *resilience—bouncing back from painful feelings, difficult circumstances and unpleasant states of mind.* Resilience is where the "rubber meets the road" regarding mental health. Everyone functions quite well when they experience well-being and common sense. However, absent the understandings that foster resilience—all it takes is one painful mood for people to "muck up" their lives!

Below is second list of psychological symptoms—most of which we all have experienced at one time or another. Let's call this one "List B." Each item on "List B" is a symptom of the "mental flu." "List B" items represent varying degrees of mental fever and psychological dis-ease. Unlike "List A," however, I'm not as interested in how often you have experiences like those on "List B." I am more interested in *how you relate to "List B" type experiences when you experience them.* So, when you experience each item on "List B," please rate yourself on how often you—*take that item seriously—become "gripped" or consumed by that item—get upset with yourself for experiencing that item—spend time thinking about or entertaining that item.*

"List B"—Symptoms of the "Mental Flu"

Directions: How often are you—consumed with—gripped by—serious about—bothered by—upset with yourself for experiencing—each of the following:

	Most of the time	Much of the time	Some of the time	Seldom	Hardly ever
1. A busy, overly-active, analytical mind		✓			
2. Feeling angry					✓
3. Having to prove your self-worth					✓
4. Feeling depressed			✓		
5. Worrying about the past				✓	
6. Having to win; be number one				✓	
7. Worrying about the future	✓				
8. Feeling foolish			✓		
9. Feeling stressed	✓				
10. Feeling jealous					✓
11. Having to be in control	✓				
12. Feeling insecure	✓				
13. Being judgmental				✓	
14. Complaining	✓				
15. Having to "look good"	✓				
16. Feeling impatient	✓				

	Most of the time	Much of the time	Some of the time	Seldom	Hardly ever
17. Feeling frustrated			✓		
18. Feeling bored					✓
19. Having to "be right"				✓	
20. Feeling restless		✓			
21. Being defensive			✓		
22. Making mistakes			✓		
23. Being closed-minded			✓		
24. Feeling resentful			✓		
25. Being vengeful					✓
26. **Not in Love with Life!**		✓			

It's important to understand that experiencing items such as those on "List B" has nothing to do with a person's mental health. Virtually everyone—even people with a deep understanding of the three principles—experiences "List B" items from time to time. Today, for example, it's only noon and I've already felt angry, judgmental, impatient and frustrated. What matters regarding people's mental health is *how they relate to "List B" type items when they experience them!*

How people relate to "List B" experiences depends on how well they understand who they really are—the three principles in action. Unfortunately, most people don't have a deep understanding of the three principles and believe a slew of misguided ideas about "List B" experiences. For example, many people think that having to prove their self-worth—having to be in control—having to win—having to look good and be right—having a busy, analytical mind—worrying about the past and the future—are helpful—even essential things to do. Also, many people believe that it's helpful—even essential—to experience anger, stress, boredom, jealousy, frustration and depression.

Many people—including many psychologists—think that painful feelings somehow get stored up in people's minds where they silently fester and eventually may erupt or explode. I used to think that my clients needed to focus on their painful feelings—experience them—release them—get them out! I thought they had to "get in touch with their inner pain" in order to be free of it. As a beginning therapist, I encouraged many clients to cry, express anger and other painful feelings. I thought that uncovering and purging painful emotions was essential and therapeutic. When a client left my office in tears, I secretly hoped that one of my colleagues would see him or her and think, "What good work Dr. Kelley must be doing!"

When people believe these misguided ideas about "List B" experiences they tend to become gripped by them—take them to heart—analyze them—become bothered by them—get upset with themselves for experiencing them. Unfortunately, the more attention people pay to "List B" experiences—the more they grow—the longer they "stick around"—the more they obscure their innate mental health.

Our culture pays a lot of attention to—even glorifies—experiences like those on "List B." Consider our popular TV dramas, soap operas and talk shows. Do they typically showcase "List A" items or "List B" items? How about the news media—"List A" or "List B?" The political arena—"List A" or "List B?" The movies—"List A" or "List

B?" Psychotherapists—"List A" or "List B?" Your company or work place—"List A" or "List B?" Your family—"List A" or "List B?" You—"List A" or "List B?" If you answered "List B" to some or most of these questions, you likely realize that we live in a culture that is consumed with the "mental flu" rather than mental health!

The purpose of completing "List A" and "List B" is to nudge your awareness—help you gauge your understanding of the three principles—help you determine whether you typically "use" the three principles in your best interest or against yourself. Perhaps some of you are wondering, "If I landed in "List A" at birth—what happened? How did I drift away from a "List A" life? How can I re-kindle and sustain the flourishing mental health that I typically experienced as a young child? These are great questions! Your willingness to consider them means that you are ready to grasp some more new insights. The next stop on our journey is *thought recognition*—understanding the power of thought and how to use it in your best interest. **How good can you stand it?**

Chapter 7

Thought Recognition: Understanding the Power of Thought

Most people don't have a clue about how people's psychological lives get created. Most people think that people's psychological experience is created from the "outside-in." Now you know the truth—it's the other way around! Everything that appears on our psychological screens is created "through us" from the "inside-out." We all live in a separate—continually changing—personal reality created by thought plus consciousness—all powered up by Mind.

Take a moment to scan the room you are in or imagine a room in your home. You likely see windows, walls, doors, lights, chairs, tables, a floor and a ceiling. It's helpful to realize that everything you see in your room is a thought created "illusion." Each window, door, wall, light, table, chair, floor and ceiling appears the way it does to you because of your particular thoughts. If you didn't have the thoughts that allow these objects to "show up" for you the way they do—you would experience them in a very different way.

When you were an infant, for example, your crib could have been in the exact same room and you wouldn't see any windows, doors, lights, or any of the other objects in your room the way you see them now. It was only after you "picked up" certain thoughts that your consciousness could arrange the "physicalness" of your room in the particular way that you see and relate to it now.

Once people learn the particular thoughts that allow their consciousness to create their personal "reality illusions," most people believe that these illusions are real or true. Most people don't realize that the way their lives appear to them is a thought created apparition. Once people pick up the thoughts that create the illusions they call doors, windows, lights, tables, chairs, floors, ceilings, and so on—most don't realize that they made it all up using the power of thought!

Imagine that you could ask a goldfish about the water in her bowl. If the goldfish could talk, she would likely say, "What water? I don't see any water!" Ms. Goldfish—you see—is so used to living in water—she doesn't even realize it's there. The same thing happens to us, humans. We are so used to living in our thought created worlds—we don't see them as thought—we see them as real—we see them as "the truth."

This important fact can be tricky to grasp. At first, most people find it difficult to "see" that every one of their psychological experiences is an illusion created from the "inside-out" via thought plus consciousness—all powered up by Mind. It's empowering, however, to realize that everything in our psychological worlds—including the chairs, windows, doors, walls, floor, and ceiling in our rooms—are thought plus consciousness created apparitions. It's helpful to realize that someone with different thoughts would experience "our rooms" in a very different way.

Imagine that you went to Australia—found a Bushman—blindfolded him—transported him to the middle of your room. Upon removing his blindfold, I assert that the Bushman would not see your doors, your windows, your chairs, your floor, or your ceiling—at least not the way that you see them. Why? Because the Bushman doesn't have the thoughts necessary for his consciousness to create these illusions. Thus, it would be impossible for the Bushman to see and relate to your "windows"—your "doors"—and the rest of the "things" in your room the way that you see and relate to them. For example, the Bushman wouldn't know how to get out of your room. If you didn't watch him closely, he might walk "smack" into one of your windows and break his nose! If you could ask the Bushman how your room appears to him, his answer would sound pretty strange!

In the critically acclaimed film, "The Gods Must Be Crazy," a pilot flying over the Australian bush country drops an empty, old-fashioned, glass Coca-Cola bottle from his cockpit window. A Bushman walking below sees the glittering object fall from the sky and land near his path. Having no thoughts to recognize a Coke bottle, the Bushman is startled and confused. Cautiously, he picks up the strange object and puts it in his backpack. Hastening back to his village, he tells his story and proudly displays his find.

The tribe members speculate about the origin and purpose of the peculiar object. They conclude that it was sent by "the Gods." They invent several uses for the "sacred gift" such as a tool for grinding, weaving and building. Soon, however, conflict erupts over who will use the object and for what purpose. The dissention escalates until the tribal Chieftain decides that the strange object was sent by "evil spirits" and orders the Bushman to take the "Devil's tool" to the Earth's edge and drop it over the side! This unique film supplies several pointed examples of "separate realities"—the fact that everyone lives in their own personal reality created "through them" from the "inside-out" via thought and consciousness—all powered up by Mind.

In New York City, 150 people from several countries had just finished the main course at an awards banquet. Unbeknownst to them, some researchers were conducting an experiment to determine how people's thoughts influence their eating habits. One part of the experiment focused on how the attendees ate their dessert—a slice of apple pie. Waiters served the pie slices in a specific, pre-determined pattern in front of each guest. The pie was placed in front of each diner so that the point of the slice faced north, east, or west. Then, the researchers observed how each guest ate his or her slice of pie.

Here's what happened. Of the 150 guests—50 were American. Before taking their first bite of pie, each American diner turned his or her plate so that the tip of the pie slice was facing them before "digging in." Then, the Americans ate their pie starting from the tip and working backwards. Virtually all the other guests dug into their slice of pie without adjusting their plate. Only the Americans adjusted their plates so that the point of the pie wedge was pointing toward them before starting to eat!

Eating a slice of pie from the tip backwards is not the absolute pie eating reality—the way some higher power proclaimed that humans should eat a slice of pie. It is simply the "pie-eating thoughts" of most Americans. When these thoughts get activated by consciousness, it appears to most Americans that this is the "right way" to eat a slice of pie.

Someone told me that Eskimos have over fifty words for snow. This didn't surprise me, however, because snow must be very important in the lives of Eskimos. Their particular thoughts allow Eskimos to see distinctions regarding snow that you and I could never see. For example, Eskimos can likely distinguish snow that's best for building—best for traveling—healthy to melt for drinking—good for preserving food. You and I would look and likely see snow, snow and more snow!

I've also heard that Ethiopian cattlemen can scan their herds from a great distance and discern which cows are ill, which are pregnant and which are in heat. You and I would look and likely see cows, cows and more cows!

Below are two trapezoids. Within each trapezoid is a simple, common phrase. Please read the phrase contained in each trapezoid.

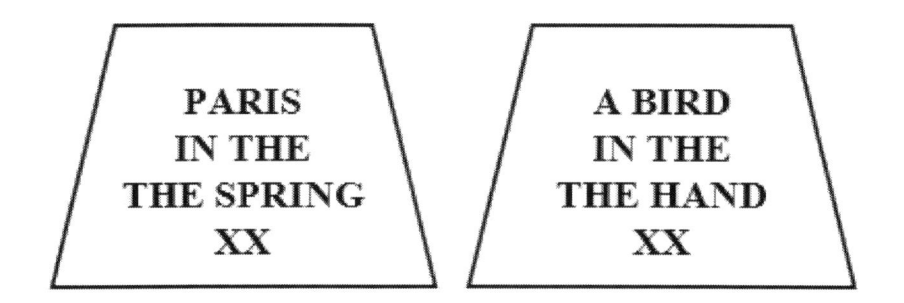

**PARIS
IN THE
THE SPRING
XX**

**A BIRD
IN THE
THE HAND
XX**

Very good! Now, read each phrase once again. Good! Now, read each phrase one more time, starting with the one on the right this time. If you haven't caught on yet, please read each phrase once more. No, it's not the two X's at the bottom. Sorry! Read each phrase once again—very slowly. Did you get it? If not, please read each phrase again—very, very slowly. If you haven't caught on by now, put your finger on each word as you read it. You got it!! There's a second "the" in both phrases. It's "Paris in the *the* spring," and "A bird in the *the* hand." The bottom line—we see what our thoughts allow us to see!

Not seeing a second "the" in some simple phrases is not the end of the world. However, not realizing that thought creates our experience can complicate our lives. Consider Meg, for example, who saw me for relationship counseling with her boyfriend, Sam. Meg's "issue" was, "I can't trust men!" Meg described several relationships, stating that in each one her partner eventually became deceitful and untrustworthy. Sam, she said, was starting to act like all the others.

I asked Meg to recall a time she felt confident that she could trust Sam. She thought for a moment and said, "Well, two weekends ago we spent the night at a romantic bed and breakfast. We had a wonderful time. I remember thinking that night how trustworthy Sam is and how grateful I am to have him in my life. I really trusted him that night!"

Before I could comment, however, Meg quickly added that such "trusting times" were becoming less frequent. Sam, she proclaimed, was starting to behave in ways that made her very suspicious.

Sam, on the other hand, was at his wit's end. He appeared to care for Meg very much, but said that about everything he said or did lately was seen by her as either a "put-down" or deceitful. Sam felt "between a rock and a hard place." Even his compliments were often seen by Meg as insincere.

After observing Meg and Sam for one session, I was clear that Meg had picked up a habit of thinking that was obscuring her common sense and distorting her view of Sam. When this thinking "kicked in," Meg misperceived and over-reacted to many of Sam's innocuous statements, gestures and behaviors. Meg's thinking created "second the's" regarding Sam that looked real to her—but weren't really there. Unless Meg understood the three principles and learned to distinguish and discount these less helpful thoughts, she would never meet a man that she would trust for very long.

Our Feelings are Illusions

Not only are all of our perceptions thought created illusions—so are all of our feelings! However, since most people don't understand how psychological experience gets created, it appears to most people that events, circumstances and how other people treat them cause them to feel the way they do. They misguidedly think that negative and positive events determine their emotional climate. This innocent misunderstanding is reflected in statements such as, "You scared the pants off of me," "You made me angry," "Winter depresses me" and "I've got the Monday morning blahs."

Imagine you are in a theater waiting for a movie to start. A few rows ahead of you a woman gets up—slaps the face of the man next to her—storms out of the theater! Several observers experience very different feelings. A middle-aged woman feels tremendous fear. A younger man feels depressed. A young woman is elated. Another man feels angry. What explains the very different emotions of four people who have observed the very same event? If the event is the cause, shouldn't their feelings be the same or at least very similar? Yet, the emotions of these four observers were very different indeed!

The answer is simple when you realize that every emotion that people experience is a "thought event." The frightened middle-aged woman remembered being physically abused by her ex-husband and thought, "Boy, is she in for it now. When he gets home, he's going to beat the heck out of her!" The elated young women thought, "You go girl! More sisters should stand up to their man like you!" The young man who felt depressed remembered his ex-wife ending their marriage and thought, "He's had it now. She's going to leave him and he'll never get her back!" The man who felt angry thought, "Just like a woman. He tries his best to please her and look what he gets in return!"

The source of the very different emotions of these observers was not the event. Their very different emotions were products of their very different thoughts. The moment people think a thought, they experience an emotion perfectly aligned with that thought. Our emotions are products of our thoughts brought to life by our consciousness from the "inside-out."

In his book, *Thoughts and Feelings,* Matthew McKay cites several scientific experiments that illustrate the fact that people's feelings are thought created illusions. One classic experiment involved administering adrenaline injections to participants who were told that they were being injected with Suproxin, a new vitamin compound. Participants were placed in an observation room for 15 to 20 minutes with an accomplice of the experimenter who "supposedly" was also injected with Suproxin. Soon, the adrenaline injected participants began experiencing typical nervous system arousal; hand tremors, heart pounding and rapid breathing. As the adrenaline took effect, the experimenter's accomplice began behaving in one of two ways. He or she either became progressively angry or acted increasingly euphoric and playful.

The participants were observed through a two-way mirror and their behavior was systematically recorded. The researchers reported that participants who waited with the angry accomplice became angry and those who waited with the euphoric accomplice became euphoric. It was also found that participants given a salt water placebo had no particular emotional reaction, no matter how the accomplice behaved. Participants who were told in advance that Suproxin often had side effects such as trembling and heart pounding also reported no specific emotional reaction, regardless of the accomplice's behavior.

The researchers concluded that emotion is not merely a physiological event, a chemical reaction in the body which automatically creates feelings. Physiological arousal, by itself, cannot produce emotions. Emotion is created by people's thoughts about events, both internal (e.g., physiological) and external. Participants in this study interpreted their physical arousal as either anger or euphoria depending on what they thought was appropriate based on the emotional reaction of the accomplice. If the accomplice was angry, they interpreted the adrenaline reaction as anger and thereafter expressed and reported feeling angry.

In another classic study, experimental participants were shown slides of Playboy magazine nudes while supposedly listening to their own heart rates. In fact, they were actually hearing a recording of random heartbeats that could be altered by the experimenters to speed up or slow down. For half of the slides, subjects heard their "heart rate" increase. These slides were subsequently rated as more attractive than slides for which their heartbeat did not change. The experimenters explained their findings by suggesting that subjects convinced themselves that a slide was attractive by actively searching the slide for attributes that might have caused such a dramatic heart rate reaction (i.e., second "the's" that weren't really there).

Later, these researchers found that people were more apt to approach a live snake if led to think that their heart rates had not increased while watching the snake. The researchers concluded that an emotional response can depend on what people think their internal state is regardless of what is actually going on inside their body. Once again, thought activated by consciousness is the source of every emotion.

In another interesting study, the researchers were able to induce anger by merely telling a participant he or she was angry. Participants were moderately provoked by two student accomplices. They were then given phony feedback about their emotional response on an "anger meter." The meter was said to measure heart rate, blood pressure and galvanic skin response or "sweating." Subjects were led to think that they were experiencing low, medium or high anger toward their tormentors. The experimenters found a systematic relationship between anger feedback and electric shocks delivered by participants to the students. In other words, participants led to believe they were angrier administered more shocks to the provoking student. The researchers concluded that subjects looked at the "anger meter," concluded from the readings that they were angry and then proceeded to feel angry. No actual physiological arousal was necessary—anger was entirely dependent on a participant's thinking that the emotion was present!

We Smell, Taste and Touch Our Thoughts

By the way, we smell our thoughts—taste our thoughts—touch our thoughts! Consider the diversity of people's food preferences. Some people think that tripe stew—made from animal intestines—is a delicacy. A "termite stir-fry" is craved in some lands. Some people devour hot peppers and Tabasco while others can't stand the thought of them. If you smelled the aroma of "asopao de pollo" cooking on a hot stove, would you know what you smelled? You would if you had the thoughts necessary to recognize this Puerto Rican delicacy. People in some cultures think the aroma of body odor is "sexy?" Men in some cultures love the look and feel of hair on the legs and underarms of women. The bottom line—every smell, taste and touch is an illusion created "through us" from the "inside-out" via thought plus consciousness—all powered up by Mind.

What We Call "Reality" is Our Next Thought

Every bit and morsel of our moment-to-moment psychological experience is created "through us" from the "inside-out" via our thoughts brought to life by our consciousness. When people don't realize this psychological fact, they view their "reality illusions" as "real" or "the truth." Also, they perceive that their psychological lives are happening "to them" from the "outside-in." Thus, many people misguidedly experience themselves as "victims of their circumstances."

That's right—our psychological lives happen "through us"—not "to us." We all work much like human movie projectors, continually experiencing our thoughts projected by consciousness onto our psychological screens. It never happens "to us" from out there—it always happens "through us" from within. We have never—ever—never—been victims of our circumstances—just victims of our own thoughts *taken seriously*!

Imagine that you wrote yourself a nasty note—hid it somewhere and forgot about it. Then several years later you accidentally discover the note, read it and scare "the bejesus" out of yourself! That's how life appears to people who don't understand the three principles at a deep level. Like dogs chasing their tails—not realizing they are attached to their own bodies—people who don't understand the three principles chase after life as if it's happening to them from the "outside-in!"

Thought Reconditioning is Not the Answer

Some of you may be wondering, "Okay—I'm grasping that my psychological life is created "through me" from the "inside-out." However, I'm still not sure how to take up residence in "List A?" Should I challenge and refute my stressful thoughts? Should I try to think more positive thoughts? Should I meditate—use positive affirmations—how about guided imagery?"

Many people think that the way to a "List A" life is to work at changing or reconditioning their thinking. Scads of psychologists support this misguided idea. I used to encourage my clients to challenge and recondition their thoughts—fight their irrational beliefs. I didn't realize then that these thought reconditioning techniques added stress for many clients—didn't help them realize the "inside-out" nature of their psychological lives—didn't help them "see" that they have all the mental health they need already inside of them.

The truth is—people can never reside in "List A" by changing, challenging, refuting or reconditioning their thinking. To reside in "List A," you don't have to do a lick of thought reconditioning. You don't have to uncover and refute any "dysfunctional beliefs." You don't have to do one bit of positive thinking, guided imagery, meditation or affirmation practice!

These techniques are another version of the "more/better/different" game. People will be happier if they think *more* positive thoughts—get *better* at challenging their negative thoughts—think about their lives in a *different* way. Working at reconditioning your thinking will never get you a "List A" lifestyle. Trying to change your thinking won't help you realize that you have all the mental health you need already inside of you. On the other hand, *realizing how to use the power of thought in your best interest* is essential. That's the next stop on our journey. **How good can you stand it?**

Chapter 8

Using the Power of Thought in Your Best Interest

From the moment we are born until our last breath we live in a cascading waterfall of thought. Even when we're sleeping—we're still thinking. Dreams are more reels of thought being projected by consciousness onto our sleeping screens. Unfortunately, most people typically think in a loud, deliberate, effortful way—as if a little monkey was in their head chattering away—judging, analyzing and commenting on just about everything. Most people have gotten so used to thinking in this effortful, clamoring way—they don't even realize it. How about you? For the next 30 seconds, please listen in on your thinking.

(Please listen in on your thinking for thirty seconds)

Well—what was it like in there—peaceful and serene or loud and chattering? If you are confused, I'll try to nudge your awareness. Perhaps you heard a little voice in your head saying something like, "What chattering little monkey? I don't hear any noisy, clamoring thinking going on. What's he talking about? This is crazy!"

At times, the minds of the noisiest thinkers quiet or clear. When this happens, their thinking changes dramatically—becomes effortless—free-flowing—responsive to the moment. How would you describe your typical thinking—loud and deliberate or quiet and effortless? Remember, our thoughts get transformed into our psychological experience. Unfortunately, most people don't realize how to use the power of thought in their best interest. Why? Because nobody ever told them the natural, responsive way that the power of thought is designed to operate. Isn't it about time that you realized how to use the power of thought in your favor?

Natural "Effortless" Thinking

Please recall a time when you got "lost" in some activity. Perhaps it was a sport or a game you were playing—a hobby or a work assignment—at the beach basking in the warm sun—hiking in the woods on a crisp autumn day. Whatever you were doing, the exact thoughts you needed effortlessly "showed up." Useful thoughts happened to mind—fresh, creative thoughts seemingly from "out of the blue." You felt exhilarated, content, graceful and spontaneous—in perfect harmony with the moment.

What if I told you that this "delicious" experience of life is available to each of us—every moment! You think I'm kidding? No way! This is how most of us typically experienced life when we were young children. Well—guess what? This experience is available to us "older kids"—as a way of life! Here's how it works. Like every psychological experience—this rich, satisfying "List A" experience is created by thought enlivened by consciousness—all powered up by Mind. However, the thoughts that consciousness transforms into this luscious "List A" experience are spawned by a kind of thinking that most people don't even know exists! These thoughts are effortlessly created by *natural thought*—the intelligent, responsive, effortless way that the human mind is designed to think.

All of us are born thinking in a natural, effortless way. Natural thought is an innate gift—effortless—wise—responsive to the moment. Our minds are designed to think primarily in an effortless, natural way. As young children, natural thought effortlessly provided us with thoughts that enlivened by consciousness had us—fully present in the moment—spend hours "in the zone"—savor each lick of ice cream—feel caressed by warm breezes—relish the flowers—become our imagining—love without hesitation—express unbridled enthusiasm—experience unconditional self-esteem. Natural thinking is so effortless and invisible that most people don't realize that it exists. Isn't it about time that you got re-acquainted with the power and magnificence of natural thought and started "thinking like a kid" again?

Realizing Natural Thought

Natural thought automatically "kicks in" as soon as we stop "trying to think." As soon as we suspend deliberate, loud, chattering, clamoring thinking—our minds clear and an intelligent stream of fresh, wise, responsive thought "kicks in." In their book, *Slowing Down to the Speed of Life*, Joe Bailey and Richard Carlson describe how natural thought is accessed:

> "To gain access to natural thought we must first know that it exists, and we must value the power of it. Second, we must have faith that if we clear the mind (stop trying to think), this mode will automatically "kick in," start feeding us a flow of thoughts—which it will... By letting go of the analytical, trying-to-figure-it-out

thinking, we create a vacuum that effortless natural thinking will fill."

When people realize the existence of natural thought—appreciate its intelligence—its responsiveness—its magnificence—ease into it—trust it to guide them—they start "thinking like kids" again—experiencing spontaneity, exhilaration and well-being as life comes at them "point blank" in each moment!

The Intelligence in Natural Thought

The more people realize the intelligence in natural thought—the more they trust it—"hush up" their busy minds—allow natural thought to guide them. Depending on how quiet people's minds become, they can experience infinite levels or depths of natural thought. At any level, people realize mental clarity, common sense and desirable feelings. As the level deepens, the power of natural thought increases. In very deep levels people often experience profound insights. At its deepest level, natural thought is the mode of genius and creativity—thought from which historic ideas and scientific breakthroughs emerge. This is the state of mind that Sydney Banks experienced when he uncovered the three principles!

Please don't worry—you don't have to surrender your intellect when you allow natural thought to direct your life. If fact, natural thought maximizes the power of your intellect! Natural thought has access to every thought that you have picked up along the way and stored in your memory. More importantly, natural thought has access to thoughts that you don't yet know—fresh, creative, original thoughts. Dr. George Pransky describes the transcendent intelligence in natural thought:

> "When we observed the operation of natural thought in ourselves and our clients, we were struck by the intelligence and responsiveness of this thinking. We noticed that this thinking gave people ideas that were clearly beyond the capabilities of their own learning and experience. Children display wisdom beyond their years. People like Albert Einstein come up with theories beyond their education that must be analyzed and proven by people with much more education and expertise than themselves. We've all had the experience of coming up with ideas and thinking to ourselves, 'I'm amazed that I could come up with an idea like that.' Writers and musicians will admit puzzlement about the quality of their creations, admitting that their products are way beyond their education and their known level of expertise. There is obviously a transcendent intelligence behind natural thought that enables us to come up with original ideas and that enables us to have thoughts that are beyond our memories, our experience, and our education."

Allowing natural thought to direct our lives is how the power of thought is designed to be used. We didn't have to learn natural thought any more than we had to learn how to breathe the right way or use our heart and kidneys correctly. When natural thought is at the helm, we don't notice our thinking any more than we notice our healthy lungs breathing or our healthy heart beating. Allowing natural thought to direct our psychological lives is the key to realizing and sustaining flourishing mental health!

"Effortful" Analytical Thinking

There is another way that people can use the power of thought. This use of thought, however, needs little introduction because—unfortunately—it is the way that most people think most of the time. This is *analytical thought.* Don't get me wrong—analytical thought is extremely useful—essential for certain tasks. When people calculate the yards of cloth they need to sew a dress—figure out the details for a wedding reception—decide when to leave for the airport to catch a flight—they bring to mind the appropriate thoughts—hold them in place—re-think them—arrive at specific conclusions. Analytical thinking is always—*and only*—useful for things like logistics, financial calculations and comparisons—anything where a known formula can be applied to specific known variables (e.g., solving a math problem). George Pransky cites an example of useful analytical thought:

> "When people make left turns in a car, for example, they go through a complex and intricate learned procedure; they look in the rear view mirror, put on the turn signal, move out to the left, move to a certain place in the intersection, look in both directions, and make the turn. New drivers attempting such a turn struggle to pay attention to and process every move when they first get behind the wheel of a car."

Many skills and habits that we pick up via analytical thought are very useful. Basic skills such as reading, writing and arithmetic—complex skills such as driving a car, hitting a golf ball, repairing an engine and doing brain surgery—initially require analytical thought. It's hard to imagine a life without analytical thought. Absent analytical thought—every morning we would have to relearn how to get dressed—make breakfast—drive our car—find our way to work!

When people use analytical thought for purposes it is designed for—right on! However, most people overuse analytical thought—and the consequences are painful! Also, most people use analytical thought for purposes it isn't meant for—and the consequences are painful!

Analytical Thought vs. Natural Thought

Natural thought and analytical thought are as different as night and day. Natural thought is innate—effortless—a Divine gift. Analytical thought is learned and takes practice. That's why young children initially resist analytical thinking. At first, it can be difficult to get a young child to attend to certain thoughts—hold these thought in mind—re-think them over and over again—to learn essential tasks such as counting, reading, telling time and tying shoelaces. Analytical thought requires that children suspend natural, effortless thinking and deliberately hold certain thoughts in mind. Analytical thought takes effort and has a "stress factor."

Natural thought is effortless. Whenever people's minds clear—they instantly access a free-flowing stream of natural, responsive thought. Whenever the mind clears, intelligent, responsive thoughts form and dissolve, form and dissolve, over and over again in a continuous free-flowing stream. The essence of natural thought is that thoughts flow through people's minds. Natural thought continues unless—and until—people intervene and deliberately hold certain thoughts in place and re-think them.

The habits and skills that we learn via analytical thought eventually get etched into our brains and when the situation presents itself, the appropriate thoughts get called up and we automatically carry out the task. At this point, learning that we have acquired using analytical thought is taken over by natural thought. For example, most of us don't have to deliberately think about driving to work. We simply get in our vehicles—start the engine—allow natural thought to guide us to our destination.

Natural thought spawns the deep, rich, natural "List A" feelings that we all desire—well-being, exhilaration, inspiration, compassion, gratitude and love. Analytical thought, on the other hand, is the source of conditioned, less satisfying feelings such as excitement, glee, pride, jealousy, anger and envy.

Natural Thought the Master—Analytical Thought its Servant

Some of you may be wondering, "If the quality of our psychological lives depends on trusting natural thought to guide us—yet, at times, analytical thought is essential—how do we use both in our best interest?" Great question and there's a very precise answer. Here's how it works. Natural thought is meant to conduct or direct our psychological lives. When natural thought is at the helm, it will signal us—provide us with an intelligent thought—to use analytical thought when responsive to the moment. Natural thought will faithfully nudge us to switch to analytical thought when it makes sense to do so. When we trust natural thought to guide us, our use of analytical thought will be responsive and productive. *Analytical thought—our intellect—is meant to be the faithful servant of natural thought.* George Pransky puts it this way:

> "As people learn, in essence, to leave their thinking alone—that is, to let natural thought guide them in and out of analytical thought as needed and to refrain from grabbing onto any thought and deliberately thinking it, their thinking is increasingly fruitful, productive, wise, and common-sense, regardless of whether it is analytical or natural thought."

While writing this book, I typically trusted natural thought to guide me. Fresh ideas often "popped" into my head. Helpful words and examples came to me from "out of the blue." Occasionally, a useful idea "bubbled up" faster than I could write it down. Old memories often came to mind in fresh, creative ways. I didn't try to retrieve them—they just showed up. Hours passed and it often seemed like minutes! If a less useful thought appeared, natural thought said, "let it float by." Often I felt like a receiver or channel through which some higher power was guiding me—and it was!

Occasionally, natural thought would nudge me with a thought to "bone up" on a particular subject. Then, I would switch to analytical thought and research that topic. While using analytical thought took some effort—it was necessary and appropriate. After using my intellect for a while, I would notice some stressful feelings—allow my mind to clear—wait for natural thought to tell me "what's next."

The Quality of Our Present Moments

The present is all that we ever have. The quality of our lives is the quality of our present moments. What determines the quality of our successive "moments of now?" That's right—it's the quality of our thinking. What would our present moments be like if we trusted natural thought to guide us? As the master or director of our thinking, natural thought would provide us with fresh, wise, insightful thoughts—rich, satisfying, natural feelings—unconditional self-esteem—prompts to use our intellect when responsive to the moment. If we stopped deliberately thinking our way through life and trusted natural thought to guide us we would experience common sense, well-being and wisdom as a lifestyle. If we got out of our own way and trusted natural thought to direct our lives, we would realize richer, more satisfying present moments and maintain our well-being during less pleasant states of mind.

Everyone has all the mental health/well-being/wisdom/resilience they need already inside of them. Unlike physical health, mental health can't be damaged—can't wear out—our minds never forget how to think in the natural, effortless way they are designed to think. Within us all—right now—is a mother lode of flourishing "List A" mental health waiting to "bubble up." Dr. George Pransky summarizes the profound utility of the gift of natural thought:

> "To repeat and emphasize the central point: the three principles suggest that natural thought is available to

all people, always, as a way of life. Natural thought is a birthright. This thinking provides the feelings that people want for themselves. It provides a transcendent intelligence for problem-solving. It provides a clear mind so that people can have an uncontaminated view of life to enjoy the moment. It even provides us with prompts about when to use analytical thinking. Natural thought is free from chronic stress and distress. It enables our humanity to come through in our personal relationships. **Natural thought is the most undiscovered and unappreciated resource in human existence."**

Now you realize the one and only way to take up residence in the community of "List A." The only way to a "List A" lifestyle is to get out of the way and allow the power of thought to work in your best interest. This means trusting natural thought to direct your psychological life. Every aspect of our lives is richer and more satisfying with natural thought at the helm. Natural thought makes any activity—washing dishes, climbing mountains, doing brain surgery—more fulfilling and exhilarating. When we experience any aspect of our lives as stressful—an "issue"—a "problem"—it means that we are using the power of thought against ourselves and have temporarily drifted away from our innate health.

Now you realize how to use analytical thought—your intellect—in your best interest. Analytical thought is meant to be the faithful servant of natural thought. If we simply leave our thinking alone—trust natural thought to guide us in and out of analytical thought—we will be "List A" fine. However, if we think that we can out smart

God—trust our "intellect alone" to guide us—we are headed for "List B" trouble!

Is natural thought the master or director of your psychological life? If you answered "no" or think there is room for improvement, it's likely that—until now—nobody ever told you how the power of thought is designed to work. Thus, it's likely that you have innocently been using the power of thought against yourself. Examining how this happens to all of us is the next stop on our journey. **How good can you stand it?**

Chapter 9

Using the Power of Thought against Yourself

I'll never forget the day I observed some children at a friend's daycare center. For an hour or so, I risked being in the same space with a dozen three and four year olds. The first thing I noticed was that each child was fully present in the moment—absorbed in his/her play and learning activities—curious, involved, spontaneous and very self-expressive!

Every now and then, however, the mood of one child or another would suddenly shift. For example, Jimmy became angry and snatched a toy from a playmate. Susie started crying and ran to a teacher. Robbie stomped off to a corner and sulked. Brandon knocked over another boy's Lego sculpture.

These mood shifts had similar characteristics. First, they were very short-lived. Each lasted a few seconds to perhaps a few minutes. Second—once they were over—they were over! Each unpleasant mood ended almost as abruptly as it began. With a little TLC or distraction from a teacher, each child moved back into healthy gear—immersed again in his or her activity as if nothing ever happened!

What accounts for this behavior of young children? They reside in "List A" most of the time. Occasionally—often dramatically—they visit "List B." Then, after very short "List B" visits, they spring back into "List A" as if their "List B" detours never happened!

Here's how it looks to me. Most of the time, young children are immersed in natural thought—thinking "at the speed of life"—fully present in the moment. Every now and then, however, a stressful thought floats down the steam—enters their mind—they take it to heart—keep "squeezing" it—they move into "List B."

Consider Susie, for example, the little girl who started crying and ran to a teacher. The thought that Susie kept squeezing was, "Billy pinched me." Sobbing profusely, she must have said this to her teacher ten times, "Billy pinched me!"—Billy pinched me!—Billy pinched me!" Susie tenaciously held on to this thought—allowing it to stagnate in her mind. However, with a little loving attention from a teacher, Susie was quick to let go of this painful thought—her mind cleared—she returned to "List A."

For most young children, painful moods are like summer thunderstorms. They happen occasionally—are part of their natural "psychological weather"—typically brief—quickly forgotten—followed by "List A" sunshine.

I left the daycare center thinking how different life would be for us "older kids" if we continued to relate to our less pleasant moods—our painful thought storms—in the way we did as young children. The time we would spend outside "List A" would be much less indeed! During our less pleasant states of mind, we wouldn't take our thoughts to heart and keep "squeezing them" like stubborn pit bulls. Much sooner we would be back in the stream of natural thought—holding no grudges—basking in the "List A" sun.

So what happened? How did we lose touch with the inner wisdom that allowed us to relate to our unpleasant "thought attacks" in a sensible way? Why as we grew older did we start entertaining stressful thoughts and "buying in" to the painful reality illusions they spawn? Why, as we added years, did we begin using the power of thought against ourselves and obscuring our flourishing mental health birthright for hours, days, months—even years? Why on earth would we do this to ourselves when it meant leaving "List A" and moving into the artificial highs and lows of "List B?"

Again, here is how it looks to me. As we grew older, all of us innocently learned to use the power of thought in some misguided ways. I emphasize that this was "innocent" because nobody ever told us—or the folks whose thinking we modeled—about the three principles and the "inside-out" nature of psychological experience. So—not knowing any better—we started using the power of thought in the same misguided ways as the people around us. Let's examine a few of the myriad ways that people learn to use the power of thought against themselves—uses of thought that obscure our innate health and spawn varying degrees of "List B" mental fever.

Modeling the Thinking Habits of Others

Many misguided uses of the power of thought are learned by observing and modeling the thinking habits of others—typically those with whom we are the closest. For example, if one or both of your parents habitually entertained angry thoughts, you may have picked up a "bad temper." If one or both of your parents was always analyzing—compulsively planning—"spinning their wheels"—you may have developed a busy, overly-active, analytical mind. If your parent worried chronically or judged and found fault with just about anything, you may have become a "worrier" and/or a "fault-finder." My colleague, Allan Flood, describes acquiring his mother's habit of worrying:

> "My mother is the quintessential worrier. When I told her yesterday I was finding time to study for an exam while I was walking the dog, her immediate response was to warn me to be careful and not trip and hurt myself. So when growing up, I learned the tendency to "squeeze" thoughts of potential danger by worrying about them - holding them in my mind longer than necessary. Understanding the three Principles gives me the perspective to disrespect these thoughts and not squeeze them as hard—to have faith in my natural thinking to look for the potholes."

Johnny, age six, was a happy child—outgoing, sociable, playful, kind and considerate. His mother, however, was "a worrier." One day, Johnny came home from school looking sad. His mother, feeling stressed that day, over-reacted. With an anxious look on her face, she grabbed Johnny's shoulders and urgently queried, "What's wrong? What's wrong?" Johnny—startled by his mother's urgency—started crying. His mother became more anxious and shouted, "WHAT'S WRONG—WHAT'S WRONG?" Johnny—really upset at this point—began crying louder. His mother frantically grabbed her phone and called her husband. Their conversation, which Johnny overheard, went something like this, "Jim (sobbing)—you've got to come home! Something's happened to Johnny. Yes, he's here. No, he's not physically hurt. He's horribly upset and I just know that someone at that school "bad touched" him or something. No, I can't get him to talk—he won't stop crying. Okay—come home as soon as you can!"

For the rest of the afternoon Johnny's mother "grilled" him about every minute of his day at school. Johnny kept saying that he didn't know why he felt sad. His mother, however, convinced that something bad happened to Johnny, continued to interrogate him. When Johnny's father arrived, both parents relentlessly questioned him and soon Johnny was enrolled in the "something bad happened at school" theory.

That night Johnny had a nightmare and woke up crying and shaking. His parents rushed to his room and while nervously comforting him, continued to search for a possible explanation for Johnny's "unusual" behavior. Johnny finally fell asleep and his parents went back to bed feeling anxious and depressed. The following morning, Johnny awakened complaining of a headache and pleading to stay home from school. A few days later the family met with me.

To make a long story short, nothing bad happened to Johnny at school. He simply experienced an unpleasant mood—some sad thoughts came to mind and Johnny felt sad. Startled by his mother's frantic questioning, Johnny began entertaining some frightening thoughts. By the time they brought Johnny to see me, he was stuck in anxious thinking and to cope had developed what psychologists call "separation anxiety" and a "school phobia."

What started out for Johnny as some sad thoughts which—left alone—would have quickly run their course, turned into the makings of a thinking habit called "worrying." Johnny's dependent and avoidant behaviors were the best ways that he could see at the time to ease his anxious feelings. Innocently, Johnny's parents were teaching him to worry and pointing him toward a "List B" life.

Overusing Analytical Thought

Analytical thought takes effort and has a stress factor. Thus, even when people use analytical thought for appropriate tasks such as doing their taxes or studying for exams, overusing analytical thought (e.g., "cramming" for an exam) results in stress symptoms—even burnout! George Pransky put it this way:

> "Even if it is used properly, people who do too much analytical thinking experience fatigue, exaggerated mood swings, and excessive emotionality. To overuse analytical thought would be equivalent to abusing the body with sleep deprivation and expending energy beyond a person's own tolerances. People who have overactive minds through excessive use of analytical thought experience boredom and stress."

I used to do hour after hour of psychotherapy with analytical thought at the helm. I seldom trusted natural thought to guide me. Heck, I didn't even know then that natural thought existed! Thus, my sessions were stressful—often draining—for me and my clients.

Overusing analytical thought to "analyze" clients and search for solutions for their "problems" and "issues" was typical for most therapists back then and still is today. That's a major reason why "burnout" in our profession is so common. Before I understood the three principles I thought that my stress came from doing therapy. Now, I realize that a major source of my stress was overusing analytical thought.

Dwelling on any thoughts for too long will eventually transport people to "List B." Consider the pre-teen girl who can't stop thinking about a cute boy she knows at school. Day and night she thinks about him. She can't get him out of her mind. Engulfed in these "wonderful" thoughts—she avoids her homework, ignores her friends and stops eating. What some call "puppy love," is actually the "mental flu" caused by overusing analytical thought.

The same way that smoking prevents our lungs from breathing naturally or that bad cholesterol blocks our blood from flowing freely through our arteries—overusing analytical thought blocks the natural flow of thought through our mind. If we squeeze any thought for too long—even for a worthwhile purpose—our mental health suffers like our physical health suffers when we chronically interfere with the natural operation of our body.

Unfortunately, there is a "busy mind" epidemic out there! Most people horribly overuse analytical thought. Most people (including most psychologists) don't realize that natural thought exists because it is effortless and invisible. Analytical thought, on the other hand, is obvious because it takes conscious effort. Thus, analytical thought is what most people view as "normal" thinking—typically the only way to think that's available. *For most people, analytical thought is the master or director of their psychological lives!*

Believing Biased Beliefs

As we journey through life, we pick up many helpful beliefs. Unfortunately, we also latch on to some less helpful ones. The list below contains "a smidgen" of less helpful, biased beliefs that many people gather up along the trail. When thoughts regarding these biased, faulty beliefs come to mind—*and we entertain them*—they cause stress—obscure common sense—damage relationships—shatter well-being! Are any of these "wild and crazy" beliefs stored in the files of your memory waiting to "pop up" and grab you?

I need an intimate partner to be happy.

People should be suspicious when things are going too well.

If I don't worry, something awful will happen.

I will finally be happy when I have children.

To be worthwhile, I must do everything well.

A good parent always sacrifices for his/her family.

If your spouse really loves you, he/she will know what you need.

I could never forgive someone who cheated on me.

Winter is depressing.

Wasting time is unforgivable.

I should always do my best.

It's important to be liked by everyone.

Life is stressful.

I must get my needs met in order to be happy.

Without a good job I can't be happy.

Laziness is unforgivable.

People should pride themselves on their appearance.

Failing at something is awful.

Painful feelings build character.

Winning is everything.

The past determines the future.

Think about a time when you became "gripped by" painful thoughts tied to a faulty belief that you picked up along the way. Perhaps it was during a sport or a game you were playing—a work assignment—a disagreement with your spouse or sweetheart.

Whenever it was, you started "squeezing" stressful thoughts tied to this belief like a stubborn pit bull! You had tunnel vision—everywhere you looked you saw only painful thoughts. The more you "spun your wheels," the more frustrated, lost and confused you became. Minutes seemed like hours. You felt tense, frustrated, confused. When all was said and done you were exhausted—drained!

Here's a winning entry from me—spawned by a faulty belief that I picked up early on and "bought into" for decades—*my self-worth depends on my performance.* It happened during a golf trip in northern Michigan. I was practicing at the driving range before our tee time. I started off hitting a few shots with my pitching wedge and everything went well. Then I grabbed my seven iron—made what I thought was a nice swing—couldn't believe what happened! Quickly, I put another ball in place and took a nice, easy swing. A wave of fear radiated through my body. It was "the golfer's nightmare"—I "shanked" two shots in a row!

For you non-golfers, a "shank" happens when you hit a golf ball and—if you're a left-handed golfer like me—the ball flies off the club almost 90 degrees to the left. I tried my best to put my fearful thoughts out of my mind. I tried to convince myself that it was "a fluke." I mean there's a big difference between shanking two shots in a row and having "the dreaded shanks!"

I took some deep breaths, stretched a bit, closed up the face on my seven iron and set up another ball. Slowly, I took the club back and unloaded—SHANK. Quickly, I teed up another ball—SHANK! Another one—SHANK!! Three more—SHANK, SHANK, SHANK!!!

My thoughts ran wild! "I can't believe this! How can this be happening? I don't shank—I never shank! What the heck am I doing wrong? OH MY GOD—our tee time is less than ten minutes away. WHAT AM I DOING WRONG?" I changed my stance—tried other clubs—adjusted my swing plane—altered my distance from the ball—loosened my grip—tried a shorter back swing—slowed down my swing speed—SHANK! SHANK!! SHANK!!!

Finally, I made my way to the first hole—discouraged, angry and frustrated. It was the worst round of golf I ever played. I hardly noticed the trees, the sky, the warm breezes, the sweet perfume of the white and pink lilac trees. I seldom interacted with my friends and felt envious when one of them hit a good shot. I felt self-conscious and was pretty withdrawn the entire day. The round seemed like it would never end. When it was finally over—I was exhausted!

I didn't realize then that I was sustaining my painful feelings by using the power of thought against myself. I thought that "playing bad golf" was the source of my pain. Dr. Judy Sedgeman describes the heavy price people pay for this innocent misunderstanding:

> "...A tennis player who moves through her game seemingly intuitively might leave the court and become frantic in the face of an angry loved one. As she engaged in more and more thinking about how difficult the situation was, she would lose the confidence and ease she had displayed on the court only moments before. Frightened by her insecure feelings, she would try to think her way out of the situation, relying on experience and knowledge,

engaging in habitual analytical thinking which consistently produces the same behavior, thus keeping her in a spiral of ever-escalating analytical thinking. It would not be obvious to her that she is using two completely different ways of thinking in each situation, and that the natural thinking that produces her experience of tennis would produce an equally exhilarating experience of any aspect of life if she understood it and learned to trust it."

My client, Ryan, complained that it was "impossible" for him to work effectively with other people. One of Ryan's college professors had divided his class into small groups to work on term projects. Ryan tried to convince the professor to let him to work alone on a term paper. The professor insisted, however, that working successfully in groups was an objective of the class. Ryan thought about withdrawing but needed the class to graduate. Instead, he asked me to help him figure out why he was "such a loner" and felt so anxious working with others.

During one session, Ryan recalled an incident from his past that seemed to relate to his present predicament. He was about nine, walking down the street with his father who suggested they race to the corner. They started running and before reaching the corner, Ryan's father deliberately tripped him. Ryan fell to the ground, badly skinning his elbow and knees. His father completed the race and then sternly admonished his sobbing son, "In this world son, you can't trust anyone!"

Not a nice thing for a father to do to a son—but such things happen. Anyway, it occurred to Ryan that he likely picked up some frightening thoughts about trusting other people. He recalled that his father was also "a loner" and that both of his parents were very suspicious of other people. It dawned on Ryan that avoiding work with others was his way of coping with the painful feelings spawned by his "believed belief"—"you can't trust anyone!" Through the new insights that Ryan gained via understanding the three principles, however, he was able to discount this belief—complete his group project—and graduate!

Then there was Frank, my client who called himself "a neat freak." Unless everything in his car, home and office was "neat and clean," Frank felt anxious and insecure. Frank demanded the same tidy behavior from his girlfriend who got so fed up with his constant nagging she threatened to leave him if he didn't get some help!

During one of our sessions, Frank recalled an incident from his past that he thought might relate to his compulsive habits. He was five years old playing in the family room with his brother. Their mother told them to stop playing and clean up the room now! When their mother returned and found the boys still "horsing around," she over-reacted and said something like, "If you boys don't get this room spotless right now, I'm going to leave and you won't have a mother!" The brothers immediately straightened up the room.

That night, Frank's brother got up to use the bathroom and found Frank sitting in the bathtub cleaning it! He quickly awakened his mother and led her to the bathroom. She immediately plucked Frank from the tub—told him that he didn't have to clean it— tucked him back in bed.

It occurred to Frank that this event might have led him think that his security and well-being depended on making sure everything was neat and clean. He remembered that his mother had "a thing about neatness"—that her favorite saying was, "Cleanliness is next to Godliness." Frank realized that when "things seemed out of order" he typically felt guilty and anxious. He "saw" that his compulsive behavior temporarily relieved these uncomfortable feelings. Through understanding the three principles, Frank realized the vicious circle in which he had innocently trapped himself. He eventually realized that his anxious feelings were really "his friend" warning him that his thinking was off. With these new insights Frank was able to shed his "neat freak" reputation.

It's helpful to recognize that our biased, faulty—beliefs, opinions, expectations—can only hurt us if—when they happen to mind—we believe them—take them to heart—entertain them! Remember, the feelings that we experience—and persist—are formed by the thoughts we choose to honor and entertain. We can't stop painful thoughts tied to faulty beliefs from coming to mind. I wish we could, but we can't. All kinds of thoughts happen to mind—beautiful thoughts—biased thoughts—stressful thoughts—neutral thoughts. We have little say about the thoughts that enter our minds. However, we have a lot to say about our thoughts—once they are formed. That's where our "free will" comes into play. We choose which thoughts we take seriously and invite in for tea and biscuits—and which thoughts we take with "with a grain of salt" and allow to pass through.

There can never be chronic stress when natural thought is at the helm. Why? Because our thoughts glide through rather than stagnate in our mind. Since natural thought is always responsive to the moment, any thoughts (even painful ones) that come to mind—come and go usefully. George Pransky puts it this way:

> "...Because these thoughts (painful ones) are flowing, they do not provide the potential for chronic stress and distress. We might have a memory of a childhood trauma or a thought of conscience that we mistreated someone without realizing it. We might feel sadness for the loss of a loved one. All these thoughts are painful, but they would not cause chronic pain because they will flow through the person's mind and actually be evolved and healed in the process. We might see a person in distress and have a bittersweet feeling of compassion. There might be a painful thought in the moment, but natural thinking protects us from chronic stress. Chronic stress and distress can only happen in the context of analytical thinking within the thoughts that are deliberately held in mind and re-thought for a period of time."

Painful Memories

Most people who experience horrid events like rape, child abuse, tragic accidents and natural disasters come away with painful memories. For many of these people, something that reminds them of the horrific event can trigger these painful recollections. Consciousness then transforms these memories into the painful feelings and perceptions associated with the original event. Consider the following incident described by a 32-year-old OIF Army Veteran taken from his blog, "This is Your War II:"

> "Standing in line at the checkout stand the feeling was almost unbearable, like a low electric current was flowing through my body, not enough to hurt but enough to make me really uncomfortable. The people behind me were standing way too close to me, their kid was making too much noise. I thought of the children I had seen in Iraq and how I never saw one cry, even the wounded ones. I felt like I was suffocating in the store, near panic, but I was going to maintain, I could do this, JUST BUY YOUR____AND GET TO THE CAR! Just then was when the boy behind me popped the balloon he was playing with. I was on the floor, clawing at the fake marble colored tiles, attempting to crawl under a magazine rack. I may have yelled INCOMING I don't know but when I came back into my body everyone was looking at me."

Liz, a 23-year-old college student was sitting at her desk on day one of her American History class. Liz was in a good mood and looking forward to the class. Her professor arrived a few minutes late—a tall, slender man, about 60 or so with a white beard. Upon making eye contact with the professor, Liz's heart started pounding and her hands shaking! She became so uncomfortable that she got up and left the classroom! Liz tried to calm down in a nearby lounge and a few minutes later attempted to re-enter the classroom. However, when she glanced at the professor through the window in the classroom door, her panicky feelings returned. Feeling "shook up" and confused, Liz decided to consult with me to find out what was going on.

After reassuring Liz that her mental health was fine, I introduced her to the three principles and described the connection between people's thinking and their experience. I suggested that Liz likely had some painful past memories re-activated. While stressing that it wasn't important that she remember the source of these memories, she might be open to recalling a related event from her past. At our next session, Liz shared the following incident that her mother recalled. Liz was about three years old, riding her tricycle on the sidewalk near her home. She hit a bump—lost her balance—fell off her trike—hit her head pretty hard on the sidewalk. A man walking on the other side of the street ran across to see if Liz was okay. Her mother also saw Liz fall and came running toward her at about the same time. Little Liz—hurt, frightened and dazed from the fall—looked up at the Good Samaritan bending over her and panicked. She struggled to her feet and ran sobbing and shaking into her mother's arms. Her mother described the stranger as a very tall, thin, older man with a long white beard!

Egotistical Thinking

Another misguided use of the power of thought is *egotistical thinking*—using thought to create the illusion that self-worth is tied to external factors such as our attributes (e.g., looks, intelligence)—accomplishments (e.g., awards, money)—circumstances (e.g., being promoted, being fired)—how other people treat us (e.g., bullying). This common use of thought is grounded in the belief that self-worth must be earned. Here's how it works. First, you select your "self-worth items" from your cultural menu. Then, you work like crazy to check those items off your list. Soon you find yourself trapped in a never ending spiral of self-consciousness, self-monitoring, self-analysis. Perform, assess, rate yourself—perform, assess, judge yourself—assess, judge, measure your worth. When you meet your self-worth standards, you feel arrogance and pride—an "ego-high." When you fall below your self-worth expectations you feel anxious and insecure—an "ego-low." Doesn't sound very peaceful and serene—does it?

I began perfecting this misguided thinking habit early on. When I was very young, my mother, father and grandfather spent hours reading me poems from a Mother Goose book of nursery rhymes. This book had drawings that illustrated classic poems such as, "The Owl and the Pussy Cat," "How Would You like to go up in a Swing," "I Eat My Peas with Honey" and "The Night before Christmas." Family members read these poems to me perhaps hundreds of times.

One day, I told my grandfather that I wanted to read some poems to him. "Papa" agreed and as my mother remembered it, "He nearly fainted!" I recited every poem—almost word for word—turning each pages at the right time.

I wasn't reading these poems. I had intuitively learned them. It wasn't intentional—I wasn't trying to prove anything. I had effortlessly memorized the poems—a natural outcome of being immersed in natural thought.

Here's what happened. My father worked at WXYZ Radio in Detroit. He helped produce some classic radio programs like "The Lone Ranger" and "The Green Hornet." He taped me reciting some poems and presented it to his station manager. A few weeks later the first broadcast of "The Little Tommy Kelley Show" aired coast-to-coast on the Mutual Broadcasting Network.

I don't remember any of it. However, my mother showed me boxes of letters and postcards from fans of the show as well as articles in several local and national magazines and newspapers. I was labeled a "child prodigy" and apparently got loads of attention—*tied to my performance on the show.*

I'm pretty sure that's when my thinking began to change. Initially, memorizing and reciting poems was natural—something that many children do because they typically live in natural thought. I suspect, however, that I began noticing that the adulation I received from my parents and others was tied to my performance! It's likely that I started thinking and believing that my self-worth depended on *performing at a very high level.*

Over time, my egotistical thinking grew from a trickle to a torrent. By the time I started school I'd created a nice-sized little ego. I thought that I had to get all A's to be "good enough." I experienced loads of anxiety during my early school years. If I thought a teacher was upset with me, I couldn't sleep. I coped by over-preparing assignments—reading each chapter four or five times before an exam—cheating, if necessary, to stay on top!

On Friday evenings—following a perfect exam score—I might allow my mind to rest a bit. For a while, I would feel relaxed and peaceful. It wouldn't be long, however, before my ego would kick back in. I'd start feeling anxious and off I'd go—up to my room to study.

The Puzzle of the Nine Dots

To illustrate the cost of using the power of thought against ourselves, consider the "puzzle of the nine dots." In this puzzle there are nine dots in the configuration below. To solve the puzzle, you must connect all nine dots using *only four* straight lines. If you haven't seen this puzzle before—give it a try.

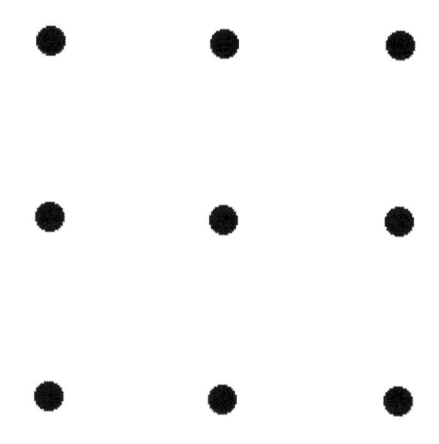

It's not as easy as you might think to connect all nine dots with just four straight lines. One dot always seems to escape. Why is it so difficult for people to see a solution for this puzzle? For one thing, most people depend on their intellect to find a solution and typically end up trapped within the "box shape" that's formed by connecting the outer dots. Then they keep searching for solutions "inside the box!"

Below, I've presented one possible solution for this puzzle. Realizing this solution, however, typically requires that people put their intellect on hold and allow natural thought to take them "outside the box."

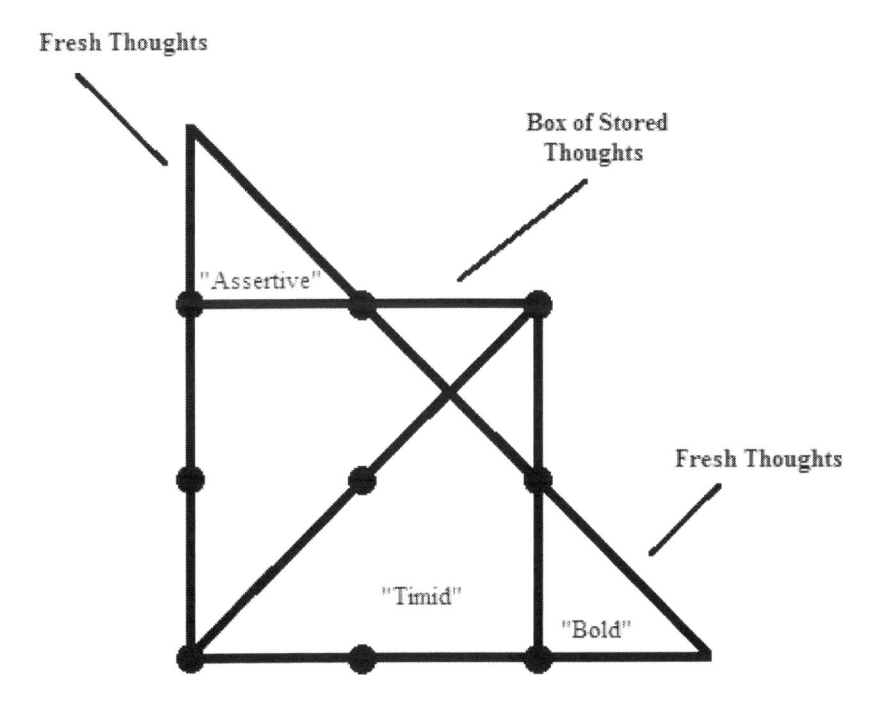

Fresh Thoughts

Box of Stored Thoughts

"Assertive"

Fresh Thoughts

"Timid"

"Bold"

Natural thought unleashes our inner wisdom and allows us to see solutions to "life's puzzles" that we are less likely to see using our intellect. Natural thought frees us from the conditioned "thought boxes" that obscure our inner wisdom and limit the possibilities that we can see. Below I use the "nine dot puzzle" to illustrate the "thought trap" of a "fixed personality." "Inside the box" is a person who believes that she or he is "very shy." This person suddenly encounters a situation for which an assertive response makes perfect sense. However, this response lies "outside the box" of this person's conditioned thinking. This person's "believed thoughts" won't let him/her respond to this situation in an assertive way. If you ask this person why, she/he will likely reply, "That's just me—I'm very shy."

The key to realizing a solution for the "puzzle of the nine dots" is the same key that's needed to see creative solutions to "life's puzzles"—using the power of thought in our best interest—allowing natural thought (our inner wisdom) to guide us.

The Arena of Unlimited Possibility

We all started out thinking "at the speed of life"—our minds free and clear—immersed in natural thought—viewing life as a smorgasbord of limitless possibility!

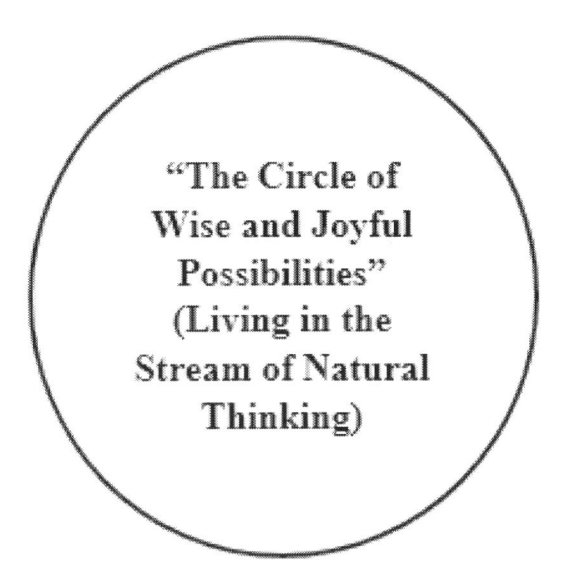

"The Circle of Wise and Joyful Possibilities" (Living in the Stream of Natural Thinking)

The Arena of Unlimited Possibility

As time passed, however, you—me—all of us innocently began using the gift of thought in less helpful ways. For example, many people learn to worry—think in a wandering, ambivalent way—"fault-find"—have a busy, overly-active, analytical mind—think egotistically. Thus, over time, people spend less time in "List A"—content and exhilarated—and more time in "List B"—stressed and insecure.

When people don't understand the three principles at a deep level, their less helpful thinking habits take on a life of their own. In no time flat, people's view of life as a smorgasbord of unlimited possibility begins to wither. Soon, many of life's possibilities appear to be "off limits"—"danger zones"—perhaps to be avoided perhaps at all cost!

The Box of Limited Possibility

Using the power of thought against ourselves and "buying into" the "List B" illusions we misguidedly create acts like one of those invisible electric fences—the kind they use to keep pets and livestock within certain boundaries. If an animal strays too far, it runs into the invisible fence and gets "zapped." Very quickly, the animal learns to avoid these areas.

With limited three principles understanding, the same thing happens to us humans. By innocently using the power of thought against ourselves we limit the possibilities that we can see. Certain areas in the "arena of unlimited possibility" begin to look dangerous. Poof—big chunks of possibility—GONE! If we don't realize what we are doing—we will eventually end up moving "lock, stock and barrel" into the claustrophobic "box of limited possibility!"

```
        Angry          Perfectionistic
        Thinking       Thinking

Busy Mind    "The Box of Limited    Worrying
                Possibility"

        Hundreds of
        Other
        Personal       Fault Finding
        Thinking
        Abuses
```

The Box of Limited Possibility

Coping Inside the Box

When people have little three principles understanding, they don't realize how they ended up confined in the "box of limited possibility" and they don't know how to escape from their often stifling "List B" lives. So what do you think they do? That's right—they do their very best to cope. When people don't realize that using the power of thought against themselves is the source of their "List B" lives, they search "out there" for ways to feel better—excuses to temporarily clear their mind—ways to distract themselves from painful emotions and unsettling perceptions. According to Dr. Roger Mills:

"This manipulation could include hitting your spouse or children, picking a fight with someone, cheating, stealing, or otherwise trying to gain more control of your situation any way you can, or it could include drinking and using drugs. It could include self-pity as an attempt to feel better or obtain sympathy. It could include violence or lashing out verbally at others. It could include escaping into an inner world through delusional states or hallucinations…The common denominator across all these self-destructive habits is that each is what the person has learned to do, or feel is the best they can do, when they are caught in the grip of insecurity."

Coping strategies are the best ways that people can see at the time to minimize their psychological pain when they don't realize its source and how to "nip it in the bud." Now you have the insights necessary to recognize when your thinking is not in your favor. Now you realize that you are "the thinker"—that you have "free will"— that you choose how you relate to your thoughts—you decide what thoughts to take seriously and what thoughts to take "with a grain of salt." Joe Bailey and Richard Carlson put it this way:

"When we become frightened, we often return to the familiar––our habits, traditions, and memories... We churn, process, reprocess, mull over, and relive an experience, over and over. This tendency is common to all of us, but it has never been productive. This is not what the intellect was meant for. Matters of the heart are generally better left to natural thought. If we can't figure something out with analysis in a few moments—or at most a few minutes—it's a good sign that we are in the wrong gear. The best strategy is to put the concern on the back burner. As we begin to sense when it's appropriate to stop using analytical thought, our intellect becomes the servant of natural thought."

Thinking like a Kid Again

I've offered a few of my clients a quick way to find a solution to their "problem." Here's what I tell them, "Go out to my waiting room or down the street to the elementary school and borrow a young child. Then, describe your problem to the child stating 'just the facts.' Then, ask the child for a solution."

One client, Don, took me up on this offer! Don was depressed after being fired from a high-paying job. He made a mistake judging the potential of a business that his company purchased on his recommendation. The business went "belly up" and his boss fired him. Don's painful feelings made it difficult for him to even look for another job. During our second session, it occurred to me to make Don "the offer."

Don immediately lightened up and to my surprise said, "Okay, let's try it." Fortunately, my next client that day was accompanied by her eight-year-old son, Jeremy. Jeremy was a bright, outgoing, happy child. He knew me from some of his mother's previous sessions and was eager to help.

I brought Jeremy into my office and introduced him to Don. Just the presence of a smiling, enthusiastic child raised Don's spirits. I told Jeremy that Don needed some help with a problem. Jeremy was ready to play and spontaneously asked Don, "What's your problem?"

Don did quite well describing "just the facts." He started out saying something like, "Well Jeremy, I had a job that I really liked and I made a lot of money. Then I made a big mistake and my boss fired me. Now, I'm really sad and angry. I'm not sure what to do." The conversation between Jeremy and Don continued something like this:

Jeremy: "Did you tell your boss you were sorry and ask him to take you back?"

Don: "Yes, but he wouldn't let me stay."

Jeremy: "I think you should find a nicer boss."

Don: "Actually, he was a really good boss. I just made a really big, dumb mistake."

Jeremy: "Well, that's okay. Everybody makes mistakes. My mom says mistakes are good so you can learn new things."

Don: "I know, but I should have known better. I was really stupid."

Jeremy: "It's okay to do dumb things. I do them all the time. Just forget about it and find a new job."

Don: "You're probably right...but it's not that easy."

Jeremy: "You seem really nice and smart to me. How many jobs have you asked for?"

Don: "Well, none yet."

Jeremy: "Then how do you know it's not easy?"

I think you get the idea. Jeremy typically lived in natural thought and often displayed wisdom beyond his years. We all have been "blown away" by the striking clarity and common sense in a young child's view of life. With natural thought at the helm, young children are often masters at seeing life's obvious and sensible possibilities. Through the lens of natural thought, a simple, sensible solution for Don's "problem" was obvious to Jeremy. No big deal!

Don, however, had drifted away from his innate health. He was trapped in the painful illusions that he was sustaining by "squeezing" his painful thoughts. Gripped by painful feelings, Don was searching desperately for a way out. However, with limited three principles understanding it was difficult for Don to stop "spinning his wheels"—allow his mind to clear—wait for his inner wisdom to show him a way.

Principles Don't Care What We Think!

Imagine that you visit your local hardware store and buy an electrical wiring kit. If you understand and follow the instructions to the letter—wire things up in sync with the principle of electricity—the lights will shine—the buzzers will buzz—everything will work perfectly. On the other hand, if you misunderstand the instructions and get your wires crossed, you will get no shining lights and no buzzing buzzers. Even worse—you might get shocked or even electrocuted!

Successfully plugging into "List A" works much the same. If you understand who you really are—the three principles in action—at a deep level—you can call "List A" home. On the other hand, if you don't understand the three principles and innocently use the power of thought against yourself—you are headed for "List B" pain and suffering!

The three principles don't care if you understand them any more than the principles of electricity and gravity care if you understand them. Principles are principles—facts are facts! If you clearly understand, respect and align yourself with them—things work very well. On the other hand, if you don't understand, respect and use principles in your favor—innocent or not—things malfunction. If you fall off a roof, gravity doesn't care one lick—it just pulls you down—splat! If you don't understand the three principles, they don't care either—they just escort you to "List B"—bam! **How good can you stand it?**

Chapter 10
The Truth about Moods

We have come a long way together on our journey. I want to acknowledge you for your willingness to listen with humility—"for not knowing." I realize that some of the understandings you have "tried on" so far differ markedly from what you previously thought about how people work psychologically. Thank you for your willingness to consider these new perspectives.

I'm confident that your humility has paid off with some helpful new insights. It's likely that you realize that our every psychological experience is created "through us" from the "inside-out" via thought plus consciousness—all powered up by Mind. It's likely that you "see" that our understanding and use of the power of thought determines the quality of our psychological lives. It's also likely that you recognize that our behavior is perfectly synchronized with the way our thinking makes our lives appear to us.

We all started out typically experiencing flourishing mental health. As time went by, however, we all innocently began "using" the power of thought in less helpful ways and started to drift away from our "List A" birthright. Then—to feel better—we discovered ways to cope—ways to ease our "List B" pain—excuses to visit or "rent" time in "List A." Whatever coping strategies we used—no matter how foolish—were the best that we could see at the time.

I'll never forget Lynn, an Olympic quality ice skater. Lynn was urged by her family to see me because she was practicing 10-12 hours a day and neglecting her husband and children. I asked Lynn how many hours a day she needed to practice to maintain and/or improve her skills. Lynn quickly responded, "Maybe 5 or 6." "Then why do you practice 10-12 hours" I queried—knowing pretty much how she would respond. With little hesitation Lynn replied, "I love to practice!" Practice was Lynn's "excuse" to quiet her mind—access natural thought—visit "List A." When she wasn't practicing, Lynn was an Olympic-sized worrier and perfectionist. Her mind got so busy at night that she needed two martinis to help her sleep. Lynn was addicted to practice because—not understanding the three Principles—practice (and some alcohol) were her tickets to "List A."

Confusion about Moods

Have you noticed how different life looks depending on your mood? When I'm in an low mood, for example, doing therapy seems stressful, my colleagues seem annoying and inconsiderate and my house looks like an old "money pit." In a good mood, on the other hand, I feel privileged to have a wonderful profession, caring friends and colleagues and a charming, older home.

Most people don't realize the truth about moods. Before I understood the three principles, this was certainly true for me. I used to think that moods had something to do with one's personality, self-image, character, physiology or genes. I knew that everyone experienced mood changes—that every day people's moods shift up and down probably hundreds of times. Sometimes the cause of a mood change seemed obvious like a death or a promotion. At other times, however, it seemed like moods had a life of their own.

Not understanding moods was a big obstacle in my work. Most of my clients were stuck in—gripped by—trying to cope with painful moods. A client might show up one week as Dr. Jekyll and the next as Mr. Hyde. At the beginning of a session a client might be mature and composed and then suddenly turn into a "basket case." With an incomplete understanding of moods, I was often unsettled—even bewildered by these sudden mood shifts.

The conflicts of the couples I saw always occurred when one or both partners was in an insecure mood. It was exclusively during such moods that these couples behaved in foolish, self-defeating—destructive ways. When I looked closely, I realized that the same was true for me!

Even more puzzling were clients who—seemingly in a positive mood—behaved foolishly. Consider Bill, for example, a salesman who began therapy feeling depressed and anxious because, "I haven't made a sale for over two months!" At our third session, Bill's depression appeared to have lifted. He announced excitedly that he had made a huge sale that set him up financially for several months. I immediately suggested that now he could afford the "much-needed" vacation that he had envisioned in our previous sessions—as his health had deteriorated and his family felt neglected. To my surprise, however, Bill vehemently disagreed, "Are you kidding me? I can't take a minute off. I've got to work even harder. I've got a chance to be "Salesman of the Year!"

What Moods Really Are

It wasn't until I understood the three principles that I realized the truth about moods. Moods are simply fluctuations in the quality of our thinking that come and go for all of us. Even people with a deep understanding of the three principles—who typically allow natural thought to guide them—experience low moods. Likewise, people with little understanding of the three principles—who typically use the power of thought against themselves—experience high moods.

A mood is noticeable to people because it's a departure from their "normal" or "typical" state of mind. For example, I began this book stating, "I used to be "normal. Like most people, I had gotten so used to living with the "mental flu"—I thought it was "normal!" Back then, my understanding of the three principles was poor. I didn't realize—at a deep level—the connection between thought and experience. I certainly didn't realize then that everyone has all the mental health they need already inside of them. Thus, I often used the power of thought against myself—over-analyzing and thinking egotistically. Not surprisingly, my "normal" mood or state of mind was mild/moderate stress and anxiety. I didn't relish these uncomfortable feelings, but I was used to living with them. At the time—they were my "normal."

Back then, a low mood for me was feeling unhappy and troubled. During this state of mind, I would entertain thoughts that were more painful than usual. Not understanding that it was "just a mood,"—merely painful thoughts passing through—I took these thoughts to heart—berated myself for having them. I mean I'm a psychologist—right! Psychologists aren't supposed to be unhappy and troubled! To cope with these painful feelings I worked even harder to prove my worth.

On the other hand, there were times back then when my mind got quiet—natural thought kicked in—I experienced a high mood—felt light-hearted—had a nice, peaceful feeling of well-being. For a while, life felt satisfying—fun—full of interesting possibilities. However, since my understanding of the three principles was poor, my high moods didn't last very long.

I'll never forget Sally, my client diagnosed with schizophrenia. Sally's "normal" state of mind was "troubled and tormented." Sally entertained thoughts like, "My husband is trying to poison me" and "I have insects in my head eating away at my brain." These thoughts spawned terror, rage and paranoid delusions. Gripped by these painful feelings and perceptions, Sally often behaved in self-destructive ways.

Sally's case illustrates that moods are relative. In other words, a low mood for "Person A" might be a very high mood for "Person B." For example, feeling unhappy and troubled used to be a very low mood for me. For Sally, however, who typically lived in a tormented state of mind—feeling unhappy and troubled was a high mood.

On the other hand, for a person who typically experiences joy and exhilaration, a low mood might be well-being and contentment. While well-being and contentment would be a high mood for most people, these pleasant feelings would be a low mood for someone who typically lives in a very high level of consciousness.

It's helpful to realize that as people's understanding of the three principles deepens, the range of moods they experience shifts upward. For example, as my understanding of the principles deepened, my "normal" state of mind shifted from "stress and anxiety" to "ease and contentment." Now, a high mood for me is wonder and gratitude for the privilege of being alive—a low mood today is my old "normal"—stress and anxiety.

Which One is a Mood?

Here's a case study to help you gauge your understanding of moods. Please don't get serious—it's just a game. Consider Michael, an excellent neurosurgeon. Michael loves his work. Michael says, "My work isn't work—it comes natural to me." Michael compares himself to a finely tuned athlete making all the right moves at the right time. Michael spends about fifty hours a week performing surgery.

At home, however, Michael is a tyrant—arrogant and controlling. He has frequent temper outbursts and often accuses his wife of not appreciating him. Michael is very critical of his children and typically focuses on what they do wrong. Compliments are rare from Michael and hinge on high levels of performance. Michael has had several extramarital affairs for which he blames his wife's weight gain. At night he needs at least two adult beverages to help him sleep.

Which one of these very different Michael's is the mood and which is his normal state of mind? Is Michael's "normal" his exhilarating experience at work and his negative state of mind at home the mood? Or, is Michael's state of mind at home his "normal" and his experience at work a mood? Which is a mood for Michael?

Michael spends most of his waking hours at work feeling content and satisfied and less time at home feeling disturbed and frustrated. Based on percentages, you might conclude that Michael's state of mind at home is the mood. This wouldn't be correct, however. Michael's "normal" state of mind is his "List B" experience at home. Michael's well-being and exhilaration at work is merely a very high mood!

Why is Michael's state of mind at work the mood? Because people's "normal" state of mind depends on their understanding of the three principles and the "inside-out" nature of psychological experience. Michael's understanding is obviously poor. Michael doesn't realize that he is using two completely different ways of thinking at work and at home. He is not aware that natural thought that produces his "List A" experience at work would produce a similar experience at home if he understood it and allowed it to do so.

Moods are "No Big Deal"

When I finally realized the truth about moods, I "saw" that moods are really "no big deal." When I recognized moods for what they really are—changes in the quality of our thinking that come and go for all of us—I stopped taking my low moods so seriously. I stopped fighting them—being gripped by them—berating myself when I experienced one. Moods—high, medium, low—happen within all of us—our psychological weather—changing as our thinking changes. That's all that moods are—really!

Realizing the truth about moods helps people keep their bearings as their "psychological weather" changes. When people understand that moods are merely changes in the quality of their thinking that come and go for everyone, they are less likely to be confused, frightened and gripped by them.

Also, when people recognize less healthy moods—painful lows and exciting highs—for what they really are, they can avoid behaving foolishly when they experience one. When they have a less responsive "thought attack"—they take care of themselves—keep their bearings—remain graceful—until their "thought storm" subsides. When people understand the truth about moods, they avoid jumping into the misguided thought currents that use to drag them down stream into Fool's Creek!

Imagine how less cluttered our lives could have been if we had realized—early on—the truth about moods. Imagine all the foolish actions we could have avoided. I used to think that I was "being honest,"—"telling it like it is"—when I shared my low mood thoughts and feelings with other people. I thought that I was contributing to people by being "straight" with them when I shared my low mood perspectives. Now I realize how misguided this was—like having the stomach flu—throwing up on people—thinking I was doing them a favor! Heck, I got married twice because I proposed both times as a way to cope with a painful mood! Pretty foolish—right? Yet, it was the best I could do at the time based on how my thinking made my life appear to me. How many people pick the wrong partners because they confuse excitement with love? How many decent people are sitting in jail right now because of some misguided action they took during a painful mood?

My client, Diane, began therapy feeling extremely depressed and anxious. Diane had experienced a series of abusive relationships. During her low moods, Diane would flashback to a night when she was so severely beaten by her ex-husband that she ended up with a traumatic brain injury! Occasionally, Diane experienced a disturbing hallucination—a voice in her head shouting, "You are stupid and worthless!"

When Diane realized the truth about moods, she "saw" that her hallucination was an illusion or as she put it, "thought trash." With this new insight Diane began taking her low moods less seriously. Now, when she hears "the voice" she doesn't believe it as readily. Instead, she often thanks it for sharing—does a little cleaning—waits for it to stop!

I'll never forget an example of understanding moods shared by Dr. Gordan Trockman, a three principles psychiatrist. Gordan described a client diagnosed with schizophrenia. During her low moods, this client often experienced a frightening hallucination—when she opened her bathroom door she would see a huge rabbit sitting on the toilet! This vision "scared the bejesus" out of her and often she would have to be hospitalized.

Dr. Trockman, trusted his wisdom to teach this woman about thought and moods. In her own way, she began to understand that "the rabbit" wasn't real—merely a thought created illusion. Later in her treatment, it occurred to Dr. Trockman to ask her about "the rabbit." To his query she responded matter of factly, "Yes, he was in the bathroom last week—I told him to hurry up and finish because I had to go!" Later in her treatment this woman, who had been seen by scads of psychiatrists, told Dr. Trockman, "You are the only doctor I've ever seen who isn't afraid of me." **How good can you stand it?**

Chapter 11

The Truth about Feelings

My understanding was also off the mark about feelings. I had "bought into" a slew of misguided ideas about people's feelings. For years, I lived my life and practiced psychotherapy viewing feelings through the lens of these faulty beliefs. Guess what? My life and my work suffered!

Consider painful feelings, for example. I used to think that feelings such as depression, anxiety and anger helped people develop character and fortitude. I used to think, "How can people appreciate positive feelings if they haven't experienced some painful ones?" I also thought that painful feelings somehow got stored up in people's minds where they would silently fester and eventually erupt or explode. I thought that people needed to focus on their painful feelings—fully experience them—release them—get them out! I believed that people had to "get in touch" with their "inner pain" in order to be free of it. As a beginning therapist my motto was, "No pain—no gain!"

I used to search for techniques to activate painful emotions in my clients. I tried to provoke certain clients into feeling sad, angry or guilty. The tone of my therapy sessions back then—heavvvy! A session might start out light-hearted, but I made sure that nice feeling didn't last long. I'd been taught that good therapy was serious and intense. I remember a college professor who admonished me during a family therapy class, "Mr. Kelley," he bellowed, "If you are having fun during your sessions, you are not doing psychotherapy!" Thus, after perhaps a few light moments, my thinking would order me to, "get back to work!" Obediently, I would change the topic or ask a question to create a more somber state of mind.

For years I was a misguided prisoner of faulty beliefs about feelings. Today, it's hard for me to imagine that I used to glorify painful feelings—see them as a way to move people toward improved mental health. When my understanding of the three principles was poor, I didn't recognize painful feelings for what they really are. Unless painful feelings can help us respond more effectively to a real and present danger—say a Greyhound bus about to flatten us—the purpose of painful feelings is to warn us that we using the power of thought against ourselves. *Stressful, painful, insecure, negative emotions are our internal smoke alarm signaling that we are drifting away from our innate health and headed for "List B" trouble.*

That's right—negative, painful, insecure emotions won't build your character—make you a better person—add to your appreciation of positive feelings—build up inside of you—spoil or damage you. You don't have to "get in touch with them" or "get them out" to feel better! All of these ideas are NONSENSE! Dr. Roger Mills puts it this way:

> "...negative emotions are not stored up like air in a balloon or pus in an abscess; they are not forced upon us from the outside but are created moment to moment by people's thinking. If clients realized this, they could begin to drop their insecure thinking habits that keep negative emotions in place and begin

to find mental health and more loving feelings. Trying to achieve mental health via negativity is like to trying to achieve peace of mind through fighting. It can never be done."

Natural Feelings verses "Artificial" Feelings

Before I understood the three principles, I spent a lot of time experiencing "List B" feelings like stress and anxiety. These painful feelings were spawned by misguided uses of thought that I had perfected—like egotistical thinking. When my accomplishments matched my expectations—I felt excited and full of pride. When my accomplishments fell short of my expectations—I felt frustrated, depressed and insecure. While my "ego highs" felt better than my "ego lows," all of these feelings were artificial and temporary. By using the power of thought to think egotistically, my life was a roller coaster ride of artificial highs and lows.

Every now and then, however, I would experience rich, deep, satisfying feelings. These feelings would sneak up on me—suddenly I would find myself immersed in them. This typically happened during my holiday trips to Florida to visit my mother and sister. I would arrive at the Tampa airport feeling "normal"—stressed out and anxious. During the drive to St. Pete Beach, I would try to impress my sister with all the "important" things I was doing back in Michigan.

For the first few days I would feel restless. Then, around the fifth or sixth day, I would "thaw out"—become relaxed and peaceful—melt into the moment—savor my meals—appreciate the flowers and wild life—enjoy the gulf waters and sunsets—feel the warmth of the sun and the gentle tropical breeze.

While I cherished these rich, satisfying times, I had little understanding of why or how they surfaced. I figured that I had "mellowed out" because I was on vacation—away from all the "stress" back in Michigan. On the final day of my trip, as we drove to the Tampa airport, a lump of sadness would form in my throat. I would be thinking about going back to my same old "stressful" routine.

Now, I realize what happened on these trips. Eventually, my mind cleared—natural thought filled the void—I experienced a very high mood. I accessed deep, natural human feelings—higher-order feelings that spring to life for all of us when our minds clear and natural thought fills the void.

It's useful to distinguish natural feelings from learned feelings. Learned feelings are "artificial"—have to be maintained—are never as desirable and satisfying as natural feelings. George Pransky puts it this way:

> "...Although some artificial emotions, such as excitement, might appear to be positive, no learned emotions are as desirable and pleasurable as natural human feelings. The emotion excitement as a "positive" experience pales in comparison to the deeper feeling of exhilaration, for example. Excitement has a component of frenetic energy that needs to be maintained; exhilaration points to the

inspiration of contentment and actually has a calming effect in the moment."

Artificial feelings can't compare to the rich, natural feelings that "bubble-up" when our mind clears. Rich, satisfying feelings such as exhilaration, contentment, gratitude, wonder, appreciation, joy, intimacy and love are available to each of us in every moment—just one thought away!

Natural feelings reflect an unconditional, non-contingent experience of life. When we allow natural thought to guide us, our appreciation of life isn't attached to our situations, circumstances, accomplishments and how others treat us—it "wells up" naturally from within.

A colleague shared an example of "unconditional satisfaction" spawned by natural thought. She was working as a therapist at a psychological clinic. One day her clinic director suggested that she change her role from therapist to clinic business manager. To this suggestion my colleague replied, "But, I love being a therapist!" Her director quickly responded, "I know—but you love everything you do!" My colleague—soon to be the "joyful" clinic business manager—thought for a moment and replied, "You know something—you're right!"

Experiencing natural "List A" feelings happens more consistently when people have a deep understanding of the three principles and allow natural thought to guide them. Rich, natural feelings are available to each of us—every moment. They are part of the package of "List A" experiences that we are meant to have as a lifestyle. Dr. George Pransky puts it like this:

> "When these feelings of well-being are focused inside, they are self-esteem. When they are focused toward the future, they are hopefulness. When they are focused toward the present, they are experienced as peace of mind. When they are focused toward the past, they are experienced as gratitude. When we experience well-being in the presence of another, it is love. All these feelings are natural, desirable, and satisfying. These feelings accompany natural thought continually. They are a constant manifestation of this natural use of thought."

Our Thought Quality Barometer

Are you beginning to see the value of understanding the truth about feelings? Our feelings serve as a built-in gauge of the quality of our thinking. Our feelings faithfully tell us whether we are using the power of thought in our best interest or against ourselves! In the same way that physical pain alerts us that something is wrong with our body, painful feelings alert us that something is wrong with our thinking. Natural feelings such as exhilaration, gratitude, joyfulness, wellbeing, compassion and love signal that we are headed in the right direction—that no matter what we are up to—we are in an excellent state of mind to move forward. Natural feelings are a "green light" informing us that we are operating at or close to our best. Painful feelings such as stress, anxiety, depression, envy and anger, as well as "emotional highs" like excitement, arrogance, and pride, are "red lights" signaling us to slow down—allow our mind to clear.

I was sitting in my office feeling peaceful and content when the phone rang. It was my friend, Dan, who started telling me about all the money he was making as an expert witness. Dan tried to convince me to give up my psychotherapy practice and join his company. As I listened, I began feeling anxious and envious. Thankfully, I realized that these painful feelings were warning me not to take this thinking to heart. Absent this understanding, I would have likely become gripped by these insecure thoughts—started believing that something was wrong with me—that I wasn't as successful as Dan—that I needed to work harder to "catch up'—that I should "close up shop" and join Dan's business. Fortunately, I noticed these painful feeling notes and realized what would likely happen if I started "squeezing" the thoughts that spawned them. Instead of adding the strings, brass, horns, cymbals and drums to an insecure thinking symphony, I stayed in tune—maintained my well-being—waited for my mind to clear. Later that day—my mind much clearer—I felt appreciation for Dan's success and realized that I was perfectly satisfied with teaching and doing therapy.

Our feelings serve as faithful guides to maintaining a residence in "List A." They tell us whether we are operating from wisdom and common sense or from ego and insecurity. They signal when it's time to slow down and allow our mind to clear. They warn us when we are "accidents waiting to happen." They faithfully tell us when we are in a "spinning-our-wheels-but-not-going-anywhere" state of mind. In the words of Dr. Roger Mills:

...as we begin to understand the real significance behind what we feel, we begin to realize that our feelings are an internal compass that can guide us past the pitfalls in life, regardless of the details or conditions that exist around us. Natural feelings (higher-order ones) let us know that our thinking is of higher quality and that we are moving in the right direction. If we feel negative, hostile, or depressed, it's time to step back and relax, to suspend struggle and judgments. If we wait patiently and allow our mind to clear, the common sense of wisdom will shine through the clouds and our thinking will be healthy once again.

How good can you stand it?

Chapter 12

Deepening Your Understanding

Congratulations! Now you understand the three principles that explain how we all work psychologically in each and every moment. Now you realize that you—me—all of us are spiritual beings experiencing a human psychological life created "through us" from the "inside-out" via thought plus consciousness—all powered up by Mind. The three principles explain all of our perceptions, emotions, states of mind, and behavior. Now you "see" that thought is the only "reality" that we can ever know and that we all have the ability to see this and be conscious of it in the moment. Now you understand how the power of thought is meant to work; natural thought the master—analytical thought its faithful servant. Now you realize that everyone has all the mental health they need already inside of them and can realize this health via a clear mind. Now you understand that the only time that we stop experiencing this health is when we obscure it with our own personal thinking. Now you realize that our feelings serve as an internal barometer informing us whether we are using the power of thought in our best interest or against ourselves. Now you "see" that you—me—all of us really are—the three principles in action!

With these new insights under your belt, there is absolutely nothing else that you have to do. The time you spend in "List A" will naturally expand. With these new insights, your hands are planted more firmly on the steering wheel of your psychological life. However, to deepen your understanding of the three principles, I'll try to "slice them up" in some additional ways.

Mental Health is Indestructible

Unlike physical health, mental health is indestructible! Mental health is buoyant—like a cork in water—constantly bobbing above the surface—unless we weigh it down with personal thought. Mental health is resilient—can't be damaged—is always waiting to surface as soon as our mind clears. With the new insights that you have grasped so far, I trust that the weight on your mental health cork is lighter. Now you know what "lighten up" really means!

We all have learned ways to use the power of thought against ourselves. For example, we all have used thought to create an "ego" or "self-image." I certainly paid a heavy "List A" price by feeding my ego illusion for so many years. As my understanding of the three principles deepened, however, I recognized and corrected for some pretty foolish behavior. For example, at social events I resisted the urge to brag about my accomplishments. I started asking other people about their lives—started listening to other people instead of listening for the next thing I would say to "sound smart" or "look cool." I began spending more time with women at social gatherings because their conversations were less likely to trigger my "ego thoughts."

These new behaviors weren't some tools or techniques that I picked up from a self-help book—they occurred to me from my own common sense. Soon, I began experiencing "being with" other people in a different way—more relaxed—at ease—enjoying myself!

When people have little understanding of the three principles, it often appears to them that worrying, fault-finding, defending their views, trying to manipulate stuff out there, playing "more, better, different" and trying to prove their self-worth are helpful—even essential things to do. With three principles understanding, however, people get better at distinguishing less helpful thoughts—not believing and entertaining them—"nipping in the bud" the painful feelings and self-defeating behavior they can spawn.

The Illusion of Problems, Needs and Urges

It may have already occurred to you that like "ego" and "self-image"—problems, needs and urges are more thought created "illusions." Problems, needs and urges are apparitions that look real to people who have little understanding of the "inside-out" nature of psychological experience.

Think about it—when people entertain stressful thoughts, life can seem problematic, unmanageable—overwhelming. When people "squeeze" stressful thoughts—just about anything can look like a problem. When I entertain stressful thoughts, my house looks like an old "money pit,"—my students seem dull and boring—my writing becomes a struggle. However, when my mind clears, my "problems" dissolve. Suddenly, I have a charming older home—my students get smarter—my writing flows.

When our minds clear—our problems disappear! In the free-flowing stream of natural thought problems get transformed—appear more manageable—even interesting challenges. When people stop taking their "problem thoughts" to heart, they are not in denial—they are simply recognizing and discounting the less responsive thoughts that have "problem mirages" show up in the first place.

Most needs, like problems, are also illusions. Unfortunately, most people tend to view life from an "outside-in" perspective and use the power of thought against themselves. It isn't surprising, therefore, that most people think that in order to be happy—their needs must be met. They misguidedly perceive that happiness is tied to "stuff out there"—their spouse making them feel loved and important—their employer satisfying their "financial needs"—the government supplying them with entitlements. Thus, they often feel needy and dependent—spend much of their lives trying to get their needs met—blaming "stuff out there" when they aren't.

When people understand the three principles, however, the illusion of needs—except for some food, water and shelter—evaporates. People realize that their well-being doesn't depend on "what happens" out there. People still see things they want, but don't live in the illusion that they "need" these things to reside in "List A." They recognize painful feelings of neediness, insecurity and dependency for what they really are—products of their own personal thinking taken seriously. They are set free from the vicious circle of re-thinking these thoughts—feeling needy and dependent—struggling to get their "needs" met—blaming themselves and/or others when they aren't.

It works exactly the same for "urges." Urges are simply "thoughts" that come to mind—usually during insecure moods—that tempt people to engage in coping behaviors that have health damaging downsides. Smoking, binge eating, gambling, drug abuse and violence are common behaviors that people use to cope with painful feelings. When people understand the three principles, however, they realize that they are not "damaged," "bad" or "sick" because they have been seduced by "urge-thoughts." They also recognize that their coping behaviors were the best ways they could see at the time to quiet their minds and/or numb their painful feelings.

Dealing with "Difficult" People

Why is it so difficult for so many people to keep their bearings when they encounter a "difficult" person? When a "difficult" person treats them in some nasty way—why do they get so "bent out of shape?" For one thing, most people don't understand why some people are so "difficult." Most people don't realize the source of "difficult" behavior in its myriad forms. This misunderstanding has people react to people's "difficult" behavior in a personal way. They see the misguided behavior of "difficult" people as a slap at their self-worth. They think, "If I don't stand up to "difficult" people—I might get "conned" or labeled a "doormat" or "a wimp."

Scads of seminars, workshops, CD's and books purport to teach us how to deal with "difficult" people. Many promote the idea that we have a right to feel hurt and angry when a "difficult' person treats us badly. Many propose that we should express our anger to these "bullies" in a constructive way. Some even suggest that we treat "difficult" people in the same obnoxious way they treat us. Millions have learned various ways to cope with "difficult" people. Yet, even with all these tools and techniques, most people continue to get "stressed out" when a "difficult" person happens their way.

When people understand the three principles, however, dealing with "difficult" people becomes easier. Why? Because when people get clear about the "inside-out" nature of psychological experience, they realize the truth about "difficult" people. They "see" that these misguided people are experts at using the power of thought against themselves! Difficult people tend to view life through biased, painful, insecure thoughts that they think are "the truth." Then they misguidedly behave "right into them."

When people understand the three principles, they realize that the behavior of "difficult" people is never personal. When they find themselves in the insecure thinking spotlight of such people, they realize that their misguided behavior has no power to hurt or damage them—unless they think it does.

How then should you respond to a "difficult" person? What if one is your boss? What if you are married to one? What if one is your child, your parent, your in-law? Well, like me, you will have to trust your wisdom to show you a way that makes sense in each situation. Trust me—you will realize a wise response if your mind is clear enough to hear it.

Depending on the particular situation, I've responded to "difficult" people by being assertive, passive, aggressive, humble, making them "right," ignoring them, reassuring them, staying away from them, firing them, calling the police and accepting them exactly the way they are. From the stream of natural thought, each of these responses made sense to me at one time or another. When our minds are clear, we can count on our inner wisdom—and compassion—to guide us. When our conditioned thinking kicks and it starts to look personal, we can do our best to be graceful—wait for our mind to clear—allow our wisdom to kick in before we act.

When people realize the truth about how we all work psychologically, they stop worrying about how other people might treat them. Why? Because they recognize that it's never personal—that their self-esteem/well-being isn't in the hands of other people. Also, they experience compassion for people who are innocently misguided. Of course, they still take care of themselves and get out of the way of "difficult" people when it makes sense to do so.

The Illusion of Permanent Damage from Trauma

I teach a class at the University on child abuse and neglect. Every year, I encounter "experts" who proclaim that child victims of severe abuse and neglect are permanently "damaged." They posit that these children are doomed to be depressed, anxious and angry for the rest of their lives—that they will never experience warm, trusting, intimate relationships with others—that as adults they must constantly be on guard lest they abuse their own children.

It's a shame that so many children experience horrid acts of violence and neglect often perpetrated by their trusted caregivers. It's essential that we do all we can to prevent such horrible acts from happening in the first place. It's essential that we offer our support and compassion to children and adolescents who have experienced these unfortunate circumstances.

In the meantime, it's helpful to see that what psychologists call "emotional scars" are simply painful memories that get etched into people's minds. It's more helpful to understand that these memories have absolutely no power to damage people—unless "they think they do." Emotions don't get stored in memory—only thoughts! We can't stop painful memories from coming to mind. I wish we could but we can't—unless we go unconscious which has its drawbacks. However, once a painful memory surfaces, we have a choice. We choose the thoughts that we entertain and take to heart and the thoughts we discount and take with "a grain of salt."

Someone told me a true story about a woman who was raped, beaten and left to die in her car on the edge of a desolate country road. Another car drove by and stopped. To her horror, this would-be Samaritan also raped her and shot her in the head! Clinging to life by a thread, she was rescued and rushed to a hospital. Although she eventually recovered, she was blinded by the gunshot!

Several months later this woman was recuperating in her hospital room. A visitor was livid—seething with anger about what happened to his friend. The "victim," however, was at peace and hopeful about her future. Her positive demeanor upset her visitor even more and he finally exclaimed, "How can you be so calm. If I were you, I'd be bitter for the rest of my life!" To this, the woman replied compassionately, "I know how much you care, but I see it this way. I gave those two men thirty minutes of my life. I'm not going to give them one minute more!"

Dr. Roger Mills, in his ground-breaking book, *Realizing Mental Health*, talks about receiving a federal grant to implement a county-wide training program for agencies working with high-risk, dysfunctional families. Many of the children in these families had been battered and/or sexually abused. Dr. Mills discovered that before his program began, these agencies had led many of these children to believe that their hideous experiences had damaged them in irreversible ways. After exposing these children to the three principles, Dr. Mills notes:

> "By showing the children how they were using their thinking to carry their traumas close to the heart, they were able to wedge a distance between themselves and their terrible memories. They learned to keep the past from infecting the present without denying the horror that occurred. The improvement they showed - in their attitudes, their relationships with their parents, their schoolwork, and every other aspect of their lives - was remarkable. When people learn how their thinking works - and thus, how to nip their insecure thinking in the bud - then they begin taking control of their lives, not re-living their traumas."

Effortless Change

I'm writing this in late December. Every year at this time, millions of people make New Year's resolutions—promises to change their lives in various ways—lose weight, quit smoking, eat healthier, exercise more, change jobs, get more education, improve relationships, build self-esteem, reduce stress and on and on. By March, most people will have given up—left with broken promises and feelings of failure. Others will "work their fannies off" and—at least for a while—fulfill their resolutions. Yet, for most of these "successful" people, their experience of "change" is effortful—a struggle—even drudgery!

Why does this "resolution ritual" repeat itself year after year? Well, it appears to me that for many people, their motivation to change comes either from egotistical thinking or the misguided belief that changing something "out there" will lead to sustained happiness. When people don't realize that they have all the mental health they need already inside of them, they try to find it by doing "more, better, different" stuff out there. Guess what—in the long run it never works!

Change motivated by ego is never deeply satisfying and requires constant effort and maintenance. Even if people achieve their goal, change motivated by ego—rather than wisdom—tends to be harsh, hollow and burdensome. That's why so many well-intentioned people eventually give up—why so many people make the same resolutions—New Year after New Year!

When people understand the three principles, however, they realize that change motivated via wisdom is more natural. When people trust natural thought to guide them, their motivators du jour include wisdom, curiosity, exhilaration, inspiration and love. From the wise perspective spawned by natural thought, people realize what makes sense for them to change and do what's necessary in a more natural way. Don't get me wrong, change motivated by wisdom often requires considerable effort. However, effort is experienced in a more "effortless way" by people who are already happy.

A Low Stress Life

Most people have loads of misguided ideas about stress. Most people believe that if you are actively engaged with life—stress is inevitable. Most people think, "Life is tough and along with the "good stuff" comes the stress. The common belief that people have to cope with life assumes that life is inherently stressful. Retirement is supposedly that wonderful time when people finally get rid of their stress and start "really living." Yet, many companies offer their prospective retirees seminars on coping with retirement stress!

Most people believe that the source of stress is "out there" in the circumstances, events and actions of other people that happen their way. There is work stress caused by job duties and supervisors—relationship stress caused by partners and children—holiday stress caused by shopping and partying—post-traumatic stress caused by traumatic events. The list of stressors gets longer each year. A recent addition—seasonal affective disorder or SAD—stress caused by gloomy weather!

It's as if there are "little stress particles" attached to "stuff out there." If you get too close—they stick to you and "zap"—you're stressed! Psychologists have developed scales on which you get "stress points" for enduring life events like a job change, a new mortgage or a divorce. The more stress points you accumulate, the more likely you are to get sick or have an accident in the near future. Most people believe these misguided ideas about stress and most mornings wake up to a "stressful" world.

When people understand the three principles, however, they "see" that the one and only cause of chronic stress is stressful thoughts—believed and entertained. Also, they realize that stressful feelings are their friend—their internal smoke alarm alerting them that they are using the power of thought against themselves. Stress doesn't come from "stuff out there." There is only stressful thought and it's not happening out there. Life isn't stressful. Your mother-in-law isn't stressful. Your clients aren't stressful. Your boss isn't stressful. Winter isn't stressful. Even a bad hair day isn't stressful! There are no "stressors" out there. Yes, bad things happen to good people. However, people's experience of the events, circumstances and people they encounter is formed via their understanding and use of the power of thought.

Leaving the Past where it Belongs

When people understand the three principles, they realize that the "past" and the "future" are more thought created illusions. All we ever experience is the present—successive moments of now. We all live in the present—we have no other choice! We do have a choice, however, about how we experience our precious present moments. Painful memories can get transported into the present and there's nothing we can do about it. However, once these memories take form—we choose how we relate to them. If we relate to our painful memories like we relate to "nightmares" these memories would have no power over us. Think about it—when you awaken from a nightmare and realize that it was "just a nightmare"—you are fine. You don't waste your day rehashing the nightmare and searching for ways to cope. You simply disregard it and get on with your life!

When people live in—dwell on—can't let go of the past—they contaminate their present moments "squeezing" past memories and judgmental thoughts about the present. They spend many precious present moments entertaining thoughts like, "It was so much better back then," "I'll never be as happy as I was in the good old days,"

"My mother loved my brother more than me," and "I'll never forgive my father for abandoning me."

When people understand the three principles, however, they realize that blaming themselves and/or others for past circumstances is senseless. Why? Because they see that everyone is always doing the best they can in the moment based how their thinking makes their lives appear to them. They realize that in each moment, everyone's behavior is perfectly aligned with their thinking. This is a psychological fact! It applies to you, your parents, your wife, your boss, your friends, your children, your in-laws—everyone! In each moment, we all dance in perfect harmony with the symphony of our thinking.

When people understand the three principles, they let themselves and others off the hook regarding the past. They stop blaming themselves and others for past actions—no matter how foolish. They "see" that blaming—dwelling on—reliving the past merely weighs down their mental health cork and contaminates their precious moments of now. When people trust the present moment (natural thought) to guide them—the past stays exactly where it belongs—in the past. Then, people can kick back and relax in the free-flowing stream of natural, gliding thought—allow their lives to unfold from their innate health and spiritual essence. **How good can you stand it?**

Chapter 13

When Everyone Understands!

One outcome of grasping new insights is "vision."—the ability to foresee future possibilities that most people can't imagine. Please join me in envisioning what the world will be like when everyone understands the three principles. When everyone understands the three principles, transformations will occur in relationships, social problems like crime and delinquency, organizations, psychotherapy, education, government, and international relations? Please join me in envisioning "a world that works for everyone!"

Relationships

Let's start with relationships. How will relationships be transformed when everyone understands the three principles? When everyone understands that all psychological experience is created from the "inside-out"—that everyone lives in a separate personal thought created reality that is continually changing—that everyone has all the mental health they need already inside of them and can realize this health via a clear mind? What if everyone realized these truths and was as clear about them as they are that the world is round? I've presented my vision below. Please feel free to add other possibilities that you foresee.

Question: How would relationships transform if everyone understood the three principles— the "inside-out" nature of psychological experience—the fact of separate realities?

Possibility: The fact that everyone lives in a separate reality and sees life differently would be accepted as a simple truth.

Question: What difference would that make for relationships?

Possibility: The fact that everyone sees life differently would stop being confusing or threatening to people. It would be seen as normal, interesting—even fascinating.

Question: What difference would that make for relationships?

Possibility: People would stop fighting with each other to prove that their personal reality is right or "the truth."

Question: What difference would that make for relationships?

Possibility: People would relate to each other from natural feelings such as exhilaration, compassion and love. They would avoided mean spirited behavior during insecure moods and quickly "clean-up" their messes when they become gripped by less healthy thinking.

Question: What difference would that make for relationships?

Possibility: Relationships would become more intimate, creative, productive, wise, cooperative, flexible, trustworthy, patient, generous, compassionate and appreciative.

Question: What difference would that make for relationships?

Possibility: People would work together in more cooperative, common sense ways and find solutions to vexing problems like poverty, crime and hunger. Ending these painful social conditions would become an idea whose time has come!

Question: What difference would that make for relationships?

Possibility: _____

_____

_____

Please add your vision here!

Social Problems like Crime and Delinquency

Bud, a university colleague, asked my opinion about an event that he couldn't fully explain. Bud was researching youth gangs in Detroit and had interviewed a 14-year-old boy who was a member of a notorious, violent inner city gang. After the interview, Bud asked this boy if he had ever seen the Detroit Zoo. When the boy said "No," Bud invited him to do so. To his surprise, the boy accepted his invitation!

The following Sunday, Bud, his wife and their two young children met this youth at a fast food restaurant near his neighborhood. During the drive to the zoo, the boy was immersed in his "tough guy" image. According to Bud, "His gate, demeanor, voice and language oozed toughness. It was quite disturbing to all of us. I thought I'd made a big mistake."

It was after they arrived at the zoo that what Bud couldn't fully understand began. According to Bud, "It was like magic! This tough kid transformed into a typical 14-year-old adolescent! His voice changed from 'deep macho' to an easy, natural pitch. His walk shifted from an exaggerated 'swagger' to a normal gait. His body relaxed and his angry grimace faded. He began smiling and showing my children some affection. The kid transformed from Mr. Hyde to Dr. Jekyll!"

Bud reported that this metamorphosis lasted for most of the afternoon. However, on the drive home—through the rearview mirror—Bud observed the boy shift back to his gangster persona. As he exited the car with a cool swagger and a "thumbs up" gesture of "thanks," the reverse transformation was complete!

Bud's story is a poignant example of the innate health that lies beneath the conditioned thinking of hard-core juvenile offenders. When this youth was away from his dangerous neighborhood—with a caring, non-judgmental family—absorbed in a unique experience—his mind cleared—he forgot "who he thought he was!" Instantly, natural thought filled the void and he got transported to "temporary sanity"—a short visit to "List A!"

When criminal justice professionals understand the three principles, their view of delinquent and criminal behavior will shift. They will understand that the innate health of chronic offenders is obscured by the conditioned thinking they have picked up along the way. They will realize that every offender has the capacity to function in a more mature, common sense, non-deviant way.

This vision is materializing! The intervention grounded in the three principles has been implemented in crime-infested inner city communities in south central Los Angeles, Oakland, San Francisco, the South Bronx, Miami, Tampa, rural Illinois, Oahu, Minneapolis, Des Moines, Charlotte and the Mississippi Delta region. Testing before and after revealed that the bulk of at-risk youth in these programs significantly changed their outlook, expectations and behavior. Levels of conflict dropped dramatically in 87% of families tested. Grade point averages of at-risk students improved by 65%. Self-esteem scores rose from the 40th to the 80th percentile. Absenteeism and school discipline referrals dropped below national averages. Teen pregnancy rates plummeted. The murder rate in one California community dropped from the highest in the state to zero—for ten consecutive years!

When criminal justice professionals catch on to the three principles, they will "see" that the challenge of ending crime and delinquency is not in trying to fix something in offenders that is missing or damaged. They will realize, instead, that the real quest is to rekindle what is already within, to draw out those inherent qualities of heart and spirit that are available to everyone in each and every moment.

Organizations

Organizations utilize scores of tools and techniques from psychology to improve employee's motivation, problem-solving, communication, decision-making, and stress management. These strategies, however, have rarely led to consistent increases in productivity and morale and sustained decreases in absenteeism, stress, substance abuse, work-related injuries, conflict, theft and workplace violence. Why? Because lasting organizational change is rarely realized via tools and techniques. To realize enduring positive change organizations must eliminate negativity and maximize the conditions that draw out the innate health of their employees! Dr. Roger Mills states:

> "...Negativity is as detrimental to the smooth running of an organization as friction is to the smooth running of an engine. Managers who feel insecure and who do not know what this feeling means and how it is produced, will focus on some form of self-protection. They will be on the lookout for trouble. They will talk down to employees, have an elevated idea of their own importance, and guard this image of self-importance with their lives. They will be reluctant to admit mistakes and will tend to blame problems on someone or something else. They will not look to themselves to discover their role in the problem. They will overlook the fact that, as organizational leaders,

they have knowingly or unknowingly contributed to whatever situation exists."

When organizations understand the three principles they will be transformed. Administrators will stop trying to motivate employees using fear, guilt, and anger. Instead, they will create conditions that draw out natural motivators such as well-being, inspiration, curiosity, compassion and exhilaration. Managers will treat employees with respect—assist them to perform their jobs with more ease—draw out their inner wisdom, imagination and creativity. Organizations will realize the simple truth that when people experience well-being—the better they perform.

Psycho-Diagnostics and Psychotherapy

Kathy was working on an advanced degree in mental health counseling. One requirement was to complete a battery of psychological tests to assess each prospective counselor's mental health.

As part of this assessment, Kathy completed the MMPI, the gold standard of personality inventories. The MMPI contains 540 items to which respondents answer "yes," or "no" depending on whether they think the item applies to them. A typical item is something like, "My well-being depends on love/support from my family." A "no" response to this item—and several similar items—is scored as "pathological." Put another way, respondents who answer "no" to most questions of this type, are viewed as being in denial of their "dependency needs"—the need for love and support from significant others in order to feel secure, fulfilled and worthwhile.

That's what happened to Kathy. She realized that security, well-being and fulfillment come from the "inside-out"—not from the "outside-in." Kathy knew that she was loved and supported by her friends and family. However, she also knew that their love and support was not the source of her well-being. Thus, she answered each MMPI "dependency item" in a manner that landed her in the "pathological" range.

A faculty member met with Kathy to discuss her "questionable" results. Kathy tried to explain that security, autonomy and well-being are innate—not tied to "stuff out there." She emphasized that although she felt loved and supported by her family and friends—her self-worth and well-being were not in their hands.

The professor, however, viewed Kathy's test results and her explanation through the lens of her theoretical beliefs. From this perspective, all the professor could see was that Kathy was "in denial." Thus, the professor recommended that Kathy consider psychotherapy to deal with "conflicts regarding her dependency needs."

Kathy realized that arguing would be fruitless and assured the professor that she would consider her recommendation. Startled by Kathy's easy agreement, the professor responded, "You weren't supposed to say that! According to your test results, you are in denial and you should fight me about therapy." Kathy calmly replied, "Well, I'm not going to fight with you. If you think that counseling would be helpful, I'm willing to consider it."

There is nothing wrong with constructing and using psychological tests and inventories. However, most of psychology's current tests are derived from theories that anchor people to their problems, their past and their personality traits and emphasize negativity and dysfunction. When psychology understands the three principles, however, most of today's psychological tests will be discarded and new tests constructed that focus on health and well-being.

The effectiveness of current psychotherapies is also limited by the same "outside-in" view of people's psychological functioning. At last count there were over 400 different psychotherapies—most emphasizing dysfunction and negativity—each espousing a different cause of psychological dysfunction and a different way to treat it. More importantly, each psychotherapy fails to recognize the principles of Mind, Consciousness, and Thought that were used to construct it. When psychology realizes the three principles, it will move from confusion and diversity to clarity and consistency in understanding the entire range of human experience from severe dysfunction to flourishing mental health.

Education

When children come to school feeling stressed, insecure and self-conscious it's hard for them to concentrate, follow directions and learn. To cope with these uncomfortable feelings, many children act-out in misguided ways. Over time, this often results in a negative, self-perpetuating spiral culminating in truancy, school failure, dropping out, delinquency, gang membership and substance abuse.

When educators understand the three principles, education will transform. Teachers will realize how the state of mind of their students impacts their ability to learn and function well at school. They will recognize how their own moods impact the moods of their students. They will realize how to draw out their student's inner wisdom and intrinsic motivators such as curiosity and inspiration.

Also, educators will recognize that when students "act out" it means they are gripped by stressful thoughts. They will stop taking the "difficult" behavior of these students to heart. Instead, they will see the innocence in their misguided behavior. While remaining firm and consistent regarding wise school rules and the consequences for breaking them—they will remain warm and compassionate. With three principles understanding, educators will create more optimal climates for learning.

Politics and Government

Winston Churchill said, "You can count on the American Congress to do the right thing after they have tried everything else." If there was ever an institution that operated in a vicious circle of egotistical thinking, insecure feelings and dysfunctional behavior—it's the American political system. Today, when most people hear the word "politics," they think of lies, manipulation, deceit, pay-offs and gridlock. A recent survey reported that the job that American parents least wanted their children to aspire to is President of the United States!

Our political system contains two major parties—Republicans and Democrats. These two camps continually compete with each other about whose personal realities are "better" or "right." Each party has several factions that compete for the advancement or triumph of one set of perceptions over the other. The end result—many innocent people suffer needlessly. It appears that most politicians would rather "look good" and "be right" than handle the country's business in sensible ways.

When politicians understand the three principles, governing will become wiser, more compassionate and effective. Republicans and Democrats will start listening to one another and their constituents. They will focus on ways to utilize the sensible aspects of their varying positions and philosophies. They will act from a genuine commitment to improve the health and well-being of all people.

When politicians understand the three principles, a spirit of cooperation will arise that was never before possible. Legislation will become lean on pork and fat on common sense. Citizens will feel supported by their legislators. Government leaders will support policies that draw out the health, well-being and creativity of the people they serve. Solutions to the world's most vexing problems will finally unfold!

International Relations

When everyone understands the three principles, world peace will be possible. People will realize that thought and thought alone determines people's reality—including the reality of a world at peace that works for everyone! Dr. Gordan Trockman, a psychiatrist who has used the three principles to guide his practice for several decades, presented his vision for world peace as it applies to the perennial conflict between the Palestinians and the Israelis:

"Suppose the Arabs and Israelis decided to start fresh. Never mind that people in the Middle East have been killing each other for several thousand years... from this day on, the past is left behind. Not forgotten, just left behind.

Suppose they were finally able to recognize that their differences arise from different thoughts about what constitutes a correct lifestyle, the right cultural values, the right way of naming God, and giving thanks - all their fighting was over different perceptions of the world, which quite naturally stem from these different thoughts.

The Arabs and Israelis would finally give up drawing lines in the hot, sandy desert, forbidding one another to cross. They would be able to see how foolish it is to kill a man because he has different thoughts about the world...we all have different thoughts. No two people in the world have the same thoughts. This is a psychological fact of life, which once discovered and accepted, brings understanding and tolerance for others with other thoughts, other world views.

The actual feeling of peace comes via thought, as does a feeling of anger. Whatever is on a person's mind at a given moment creates their feelings at that moment. Peace is only a thought away...it depends on letting go of negative thoughts, memories, and beliefs from the past. After all, such thoughts and memories are only as important as the person thinking about them thinks they are.

Imagine two teams, the Arabs and Israelis; from the higher elevations, they could bring water down to irrigate the desert. They could hold a competition to see which team grows the most food. The team that won would have the honor of giving the festival at the end of the season. At first, these high-spirited teams might look at the other team working and make fun, perhaps laughing about the way the others dress. 'Look at those long robes, they are really setting themselves back with all that clothing.' Then they would notice, 'Oh, they can work a half hour longer in the sun than we can because they dress like that... maybe we should try it, or they are going to win the contest.'

They would start to learn from each other. They would see that with co-operation, all can co-exist in peace. All their energy would go into constructive activities. No more energy wasted on negativity and violence. At the end of the season, they would probably have food left over, which could be sent to hungry children somewhere else in the world.

All it would take for this to happen is for a sufficient number of people in the region to realize how thought works. Thought creates our reality from within our own minds. People create their perception of the world from their thinking, then step out into the world to play the game of life according to the way they see it...they don't see a single 'reality,' they see 'a reality.' A man or woman always has the ability to change his or her mind. A small change, but a giant leap for the evolution of the human race."

The value of understanding the three principles for individuals, couples, families, educators, psychologists, organizations and nations is incalculable. As more and more people understand the three principles, the possibility of "a world that works for everyone" will become "an idea whose time has come." I know that many of you are eager to contribute to this vision. Through the new insights that you have grasped via understanding the three principles, you are creating this future now! **How good can you stand it?**

Epilogue
Making a Difference

The end of our journey is at hand. It has been a privilege being your coach! Thank you for allowing me to introduce you to the real you—the three principles in action. During our time together, my understanding of the three principles has deepened considerably. Thank-you for coaching me!

Another by-product of grasping new insights is the desire to share them with others—to make a difference in their lives. Through the insights that people gain through understanding the three principles their lives show up as precious gifts to be cherished and savored—the scent of lilacs in the spring—the smell of burning leaves on a crisp fall day—the touch of a friend's hand on the shoulder—an ice cream cone—a gentle breeze—a kiss on the cheek from a small child. Understanding the three principles transforms people's lives and over time will lead to a world that works for everyone!

How good can you stand it? Please don't worry—with the new insights you have grasped via understanding the three principles...

YOU WILL STAND IT AS GOOD AS IT GETS!!!

Personal Coaching and Additional Three Principles Resources

Three Principles Psychotherapy/Coaching with Tom Kelley:

Thomas M. Kelley, Ph.D.
Licensed Psychologist
Reflections Counseling Center
2888 E. Long Lake Rd., Suite #170
Troy, MI 48085
248-227-1757

Three Principles Research by Tom Kelley and Associates

Kelley, T. M., Pransky, J., & Lambert, E (In Press). Realizing improved mental health through understanding three spiritual principles. *Spirituality in Clinical Practice,*

Kelley, T. M., Pransky, J. & Lambert, E. (2015). Inside-out or outside-in: Understanding spiritual principles or depending on techniques to realize improved mindfulness/mental health. *Journal of Spirituality in Mental Health,* DOI: 10.1080/19349637.2014.998752.

Kelley, T. M., Pransky, J., & Sedgeman, J. (2014). Principles for realizing resilience in trauma exposed juvenile offenders: A promising new intervention for juvenile justice professionals. *Journal of Child and Adolescent Trauma,* DOI 10.1007/s40653-014-0018-8

Pransky, J., & Kelley, T. M. (2014). Three principles for realizing mental health: A new psycho-spiritual view. *Journal of Creativity in Mental Health, 9*, 53-68.

Kelley, T. M., & Pransky, J. (2013). Principles for realizing health: A new view of trauma and human resilience. *Journal of Traumatic Stress Disorders and Treatment,* 2, 1, doi.org/10.4172/2324-8947.1000102

Kelley, T. M., & Lambert, E. (2012). Mindfulness as a potential means of attenuating anger and aggression for prospective criminal justice professionals. *Mindfulness. 3*(4), 261-274.

Kelley, T. M. (2011). Thought recognition and psychological well-being: An empirical test of principle-based correctional counseling. *Counseling and Psychotherapy Research. 11*(2), *140-147.*

Kelley, T. M. (2008). Principle-based correctional counseling: Teaching health versus treating illness. *Applied Psychology in Criminal Justice,* 4 (2), 182-202.

Kelley, T. M., Mills, Roger C., & Shuford, Rita (2005). A principle-based psychology of school violence prevention. *Journal of School Violence,* 4, 2, 47-73.

Kelley, T. M. (2005). Mental health and prospective police professionals. *Policing: An International Journal of Police Strategies and Management,* 4, 1, 6-27.

Kelley, T. M. (2005). Innate mental health and resilience. *American Psychologist,* 60, 3, 265.

Kelley, T. M. (2004). Positive psychology and adolescent mental health: False promise or true breakthrough? *Adolescence,* 39, 154, 257-278.

Kelley, T. M. (2003). Preventing youth violence through Health Realization. *Youth Violence and Juvenile Justice,* 1, 4, 369-387.

Kelley, Thomas M. (2003). Health realization: A Principle-based psychology of positive youth development. *Child and Youth Care Forum,* 32, 1, 47-72.

Kelley, T. M. (2001). The need for a principle-based positive psychology. *American Psychologist,* 56, 1, 36-37.

Kelley, T. M., & Stack, S. A. (2000). Thought recognition, locus of control, and adolescent well-being. *Adolescence,* 25, 139, 531-550.

Kelley, T. M. (1996). At-risk youth and locus of control: Do they really see a choice? *Juvenile and Family Court Journal,* 47, 4, 39-54.

Kelley, Thomas M. (1996). A critique of social bonding and control theory of delinquency using the principles of Psychology of Mind. *Adolescence,* 31, 122, 321-327.

Kelley, T. M. (1993). Crime and Psychology of Mind: A neo-cognitive view of delinquency. In G. Barak (Ed.) *Varieties of criminology: Readings from a dynamic discipline.* Prager.

Kelley, T. M. (1993). Neo-cognitive learning theory: Implications for prevention and early intervention strategies with at-risk youth. *Adolescence,* 28, 110, 439-460.

Kelley, T. M. (1993). An advanced criminology based on Psychology of Mind. *Offender Rehabilitation,* 19, 173-190.

Kelley, T. M. (1990). A neo-cognitive model of crime. *Offender Rehabilitation,* 16, 1-26.

Other Three Principles Books

Second Chance by Sydney Banks

Dear Lisa by Sydney Banks

The Missing Link by Sydney Banks

The Enlightened Gardener by Sydney Banks

The Enlightened Gardener Revisited by Sydney Banks

Realizing Mental Health by Roger Mills

The Relationship Handbook by George Pransky

The Wisdom Within by Roger Mills and Elsie Spittle

Prevention from the Inside-Out by Jack Pransky

Modello: A Story of Hope for the Inner City and Beyond by Jack Pransky

Somebody Should Have Told Us by Jack Pransky

Parenting from the Heart by Jack Pransky

What is a Thought: A Thought is A Lot by Jack Pransky

Being Human by Amy Johnson

The Little Book of Big Change by Amy Johnson

Our True Identity...The Three Principles by Elsie Spittle

The Inside-Out Revolution by Michael Neil

Slowing Down to the Speed of Life by Joseph Bailey and Richard Carlson

Instant Motivation by Chantel Burns

State of Mind in the Classroom by Ami Chen Mills-Naim

Invisible Power: Insight Principles and Work by Ken Manning, Robin Charbit, Sandy Krot

Three Principles Websites

Three Principles Global Community: A non-profit organization committed to bringing the Three Principles understanding to people throughout the world.

Three Principles Movies: Videos, trainings and research regarding the Three Principles.

Three Principles Living: To inspire others to find their own natural well-being and bring their understanding into their life and work.

Center for Inside-Out Understanding: Books, trainings and videos grounded in the three Principles

Center for Sustainable Change: A global non-profit, dedicated to promoting an understanding of the principles of Mind, Consciousness and Thought as the essential curriculum for all learners.

The Three Principles Foundation: A not-for-profit organization dedicated to sharing the Principles of Mind, Consciousness and Thought as taught by Sydney Banks, and to preserving them in their purest and most powerful form.

Printed in Great Britain
by Amazon